For Black women, achieving professional success can seem like an impossible mountain to climb. But, it doesn't have to be, IF you have the right attitude AND the right climbing tools. In **Work It, Girl! The Black Woman's Guide to Professional Success**, you'll get just that. As a Black woman, you will realize that you DO have the strength to succeed.

This guide will keep it real by acknowledging the hundreds of 'justifications' we use to stay stuck where we are, but it will also debunk the myths of career choice (or lack thereof). It will recognize that we all have limitations, yet it will present 'doable' work options for Sisters who think there are none. Finally, it will not preach to the choir, but instead describe practical steps you can take to get where you want to be—even if you are not yet sure where that is!

When frustration about your professional standing makes you want to sing the words of a classic gospel song: "You don't have to move the mountain, but give me the strength to climb," you'll love reading about the experiences of incredible Sisters who not only found their strength to climb, but who also enjoyed the ascent. We know we can't move the mountains, but we want to prepare you for a wonderful climb. So, let's **work it, girl!!**

Work It, Girl!

The Black Woman's Guide to Professional Success

Lorraine Morris Cole &
Pamela M. McBride

Parker Publishing, LLC

She Ready! is an imprint of Parker Publishing, LLC.

Published by Parker Publishing, LLC
12523 Limonite Avenue, Suite #440-245
Mira Loma, California 91752
www.parker-publishing.com

ISBN: 978-1-60043-023-7
First Edition

Manufactured in the United States of America

Cover Design by Mariondesigns.com

Lorraine's Cover Photo: Horace Landrum – Landrum Photography
Pamela's Cover Photo: Neal Long – Pegasus Services Photography

The affiliation of Claire McIntosh (Foreword) is provided for identifica-
tion purposes only and does not represent an endorsement.

Dedications

Lorraine's Dedication:
To my beloved father, David "Pop" Morris, who departed this life on August 11, 2005.

Pamela's dedication:
For those who make me who I am: Doug, Tré, Taylor, Pat, Dad, and Mom.

Acknowledgements

Lorraine's Acknowledgements:
If my life ends tomorrow always know that I was uniquely and truly blessed to have the love and support of many people. I will attempt to thank as many of you as I can, knowing that my true list could fill an entire book:

Thank you God for answering my prayers!

My father, the late David Morris, for his discipline and love - forever in my heart.

My mother, Emma (Larke) Morris Glover and Leroy Glover for your love and support. Mom, you are a wonderful person with a heart of gold!

My husband, Brian Cole Sr., who has joined me on the journey of love and life. May we be all that we can be!

Brian Cole Jr. (BJ)—My greatest wish for you is that you reach your full potential.

Hayley Larke Cole and Evan Morris Cole—Giving birth to you has been my greatest accomplishment. You are my gifts.

My sister, Penny Morris Young, for being a truly special person. Much love to the Young Crew– Dale, D'andra, D.J. and Dayjah.

My sister Marvel, and Mike, Bruce and Brink.

My best friend, Tamla Tymus Scott, for being such a good friend to me.

(Love to Tyler and Eric and the entire Tymus Family.)

My aunts and uncles: Teresa (George) Pope; Shirley (Moses) Johnson; Elaine (Haywood) Massenburg; Alvin (Pat) Larke; Charles Larke; Johnnie (Barbara) Larke; Edith Larke; Yetive Larke; George Larke; Warren Larke; Dorothy Lockhart; Mary (Howard) Shelton; Gertrude (Russell) Small; the late John and Elijah Morris—all of their children and grandchildren. My extended family: Dunbar and Aaron.

My grandparents: Alvin Sr. and the late Staretha Larke; the late John and Lucille Morris. My Godparents: Warren and Edna Aaron & Vernon and Gladys Johnson.

The families that I married into: Cole, Dore, McIntyre, McAfee, Rowe, and Mann. Especially Mama (Geneva) Cole, Rhonda, Charles Jr. (June Bug), Cherisa and Glen.

Sabrina McAfee – We are more than cousin-in-laws – God has made us great friends and fellow writers. Thanks for all your love and support! (www.writeonbooks.net)

My cousin Felicia (Lit) Pinkston who is like a cousin, sister and friend all wrapped into one!

My sister circle: Shawn Craig Parker (my goal partner), Dana Legette Traylor, JaQuitta (sangin')Williams, Michele Johnson Cardwell, Angela Chandler Sneed, DeAnna Risher, Jonelle Mason, Angela Lefft Dunn, LaTasha Cook, Lisa Harden Fields, Lisa Williams Holloway, Rhonda Davenport, Carla Thomas (the stylist for my hair on the book cover), Val McKnight, Dartrice White, Ramona Roman, Linda M. Ferguson, ET ATL Crew: J.J. Spann, Della Stephens, Kym Dula, DLT— I have been so blessed I can't name all of you!

The Epsilon Theta Chapter of Delta Sigma Theta Sorority Incorporated (especially Spring 90) and two of my NSU Delta mentors, Phyllis Coley and Wanda Brockington.

Norfolk State University – GO SPARTANS!

My radio friends: Minnesota Fattz, Cher Best, Gena Lavigne, P.C., Mighty Peanut, Derrick Jonzun and the late Carroll Redd, Rick Eaves and Robert Taylor.

My military families: White, Inabinett, Mason, Hearn, Underwood, Deville, Oates, Garfield, Cornick, Jones, Conyers—you have made the moves not only bearable, but fun.

Greater Young Zion (GYZ), my church home, and our great leader William Blount for spiritual guidance. My "uncle minister" – Rev. Dr. Alvin Larke Jr. for so much love. My Virginia church- First Mount Zion.

Author extraordinaire Kimberla Lawson Roby who has embraced me and my work –all the best to you. Keep on giving us a great read!

Mocha Moms –the national organization and the Augusta and Woodbridge chapters.

To Drs. Shirley A.R. Lewis and Vivian Pennamon – it was my pleasure to work for you both and watch you *work it*.

For every publication that has allowed me to get my "write" on! A special thanks to Mr. Benjamin at *City Tribune* for allowing me to become a columnist.

A special and sincere thank you to Mr. & Mrs. Horace Landrum (Landrum Photography) for my cover photo. You are the best!

Last, but definitely not least, my writing partner Pamela M. McBride: WE DID IT! It's really amazing how we have been able to work it! Thanks for sharing this dream with me.

To everyone that I have not named. Thanks for whatever you brought to my life journey.

Peace and Much Love! –Lorraine Morris Cole

Pamela's Acknowledgements:

Wow, I cannot believe the time has finally come for this dream to be realized.

I never set out to be a writer, but I thank God that He steered me in that direction, a little at a time, without the pressure of having to making a living at it. Thank God for bringing people and situations into my life at the right time, because timing has been everything! Speaking of which: one more thanks to God for the impeccable timing of Doug's and my paths crossing.

Doug, you have been an incredibly supportive husband and an awesome Dad to our two outstanding children. Thanks for encouraging me to pursue my writing passion just because I loved it so much.

Thanks to my children Tré and Taylor who gave me such heart-felt things to write about and who loved to see Mommy's name and photo in the magazines.

Thanks Dad, Jerry Edwards, for being there and for being you. We are so happy that you now live close enough to see us everyday. You are and always have been one of my biggest cheerleaders. Your pride in me means the world.

Thanks to my sister Pat Ussery. For so many years you have been a ROCK to me. Talking to you nearly every single day no matter what state is my home has truly become a necessity for me. I love you!

To Mom, Audrey Miller, you not only read everything I wrote, but told everyone you know to do the same. Thanks for being so interested in my writing.

To my grandparents, the late Jesse & Mary Edwards, the late Lowery Miller, Verie Miller, the late Essie Stovall, and all my aunts, and uncles, I am so glad you had a strong presence in my life!

To the late Douglas McBride, Sr, for being wonderful from day one. We miss you dearly. Even Taylor somehow knows how wonderful 'Pop Pop' was and she never had the chance to meet you.

To Betty McBride, a mother-in-law like no other, thanks for all you do for the rest of the clan.

To my cousins, I love you with all my heart.

To my nieces, nephews, and 'little' cousins', I love you even more. Stay strong and grow into wonderful, good-hearted, caring adults.

To Claire Morris, who not only introduced me to freelance writing, but who taught me how to break into it with the right tool: the dreaded query letter!

To Ken Morgan, who hired me as a career counselor in 1993 and provided much professional guidance.

To Chuck Bussey, thanks for your input into my professional development as I relocated, and relocated, and relocated over the years.

Thanks to Tonja, Nathan, and Makayla Zeigler for always asking how the book was going and for urging me to let the girls play together so I could get some work done on it.

To Lynette and Juanita, my silent cheerleaders, thanks for all you said and all you didn't say.

Melissa, thanks for letting me run ideas past you and for helping me make connections that really counted!

To every editor whose repeated assignments have shaped my writing career, including Lena Sherrod (Essence), Robert Miller (Black Collegian), Kitty Pope & Leslie Royal (Upscale), Regina Galvin (Army Times & Military Spouse Magazine), and others.

To my Sorors of Alpha Kappa Alpha Sorority, Inc. and my military family far and near, you are a special part of me and I am truly glad to be a part of you.

To all my family, friends, and colleagues who are waiting for the day this book 'hits the streets': it's out and it's time to rack up on the copies of it. Pass it on.

Thanks in advance to every reader who will buy and read this book. Here's to you and a lifetime of *working it!*

Lorraine, you are truly a great partner. It's amazing how we clicked right from the start. We were the perfect partnership: we thought enough alike for the project to have been smooth sailing, but also differently enough for all views to be well-represented. Girl, we truly *worked it!*

With Sincerity,

Pamela M. McBride

Acknowledgements from Lorraine and Pamela:

We would like to thank Jonelle Mason for introducing us. Without her, there would be no *Work It, Girl!* collaboration.

Thanks to Deatri King-Bey who believed in our project from the first read!

It has "taken a village" to get this book into the hands of readers. The process started with Angelique Justin, Cheysa, Genice and others and after some transitions was then taken on by Miriam Pace and others in the Parker family. We are grateful to each and every one of you.

Thanks to every woman who contributed to this book. You shared your experiences unselfishly and provided a blueprint for our readers on their path to success. Thanks for your knowledge and willingness to share it. You all are truly women who *work it!*

Table of Contents

WORK IT, GIRL!
Foreword by Claire McIntosh,
Deputy Editor of ESSENCE Magazine

Years before I got my job at ESSENCE, I worked for another major women's magazine geared toward a "general market" audience. I was one of just two African-American editors on a staff of more than thirty. Once during a story-planning meeting, a couple of our White coworkers had a brainstorm—why don't we publish a feature on Black women? Others in the group agreed—yes, yes this is something we need to write about. The problem was, that's not a story, it's a demographic. When pressed to narrow down their focus to what they felt was truly remarkable and noteworthy to say about Black women, they fumbled a bit, not quite being able to articulate clearly for a while. I remember names of successful women like Oprah Winfrey and Terry McMillan being tossed out. But what eventually was distilled from that brainstorming session was this: Witnessing so many of us Sisters running companies or running for Congress, rising from oppression to empowerment or from obscurity to mega-success, they felt that there was some special strength we had as a group. Some secret formula for success was propelling many of us to greatness at the turn of a new millennium. And they wanted to know how to tap into it.

That story never ran. But the incident left an impression on me and the other Sister I worked with. Would we have ever pitched such a story? Probably not. That Black women at all levels of society have what you might call a "striving gene" is something most of us take for granted. Apparently, others don't.

Of course, Black women are as diverse as we are determined, so while most of us are "working it" in some way or another, we probably won't all agree about what "it" is. But for a lot of us, there's a deep spirituality that drives our professional lives. I can't tell you the number of African-American women I've interviewed over the years for ESSENCE articles on career success who consider prayer as essential as a power suit, or meditation as necessary as a mentor. Many at the top of their profession speak of using "spiritual warfare" to break down barriers in government, academia, entertainment or Corporate America. That faith is so central to who we are at work is unique to us, I believe, whether we express it by using "Psalm 23" as our e-mail password or by sending thoughts of loving kindness, in the Buddhist tradition, to the unseen person at the other end of a ringing office phone.

For others, "it" means that we're working for something larger than a paycheck.

Depending on our success, we support our sons and daughters, parents and grandparents, clubs and committees, churches and schools, candidates and causes, neighbors and faraway families in need. We are driven by a sense of collective well-being that spans generations.

And speaking of generations, we're also driven by a legacy. Mothers, grandmothers and great-great-great aunts worked with a lot less than we have and made a way out of no way. Those strong women we've grown accustomed to seeing all around us are part of the reason we sometimes take "it" for granted. When I look at many of the themes explored in this book, I think of my own Mom. She had not one but several careers she was passionate about—registered nurse, science teacher, assistant principal, camp counselor. And she hustled a few antiques on the side, turning her hobby into an additional source of income. Ina Reynolds McIntosh taught her five daughters that we could have it all—just not all at once.

She took periods of time off to raise her children and enlisted household help when she reentered the workforce. And sometimes the dreams she dreamed for her children meant that she deferred some of her own— becoming a writer, for instance. But at eighty-one she's enrolled in a workshop and putting her thoughts on paper. Those passions she didn't fully pursue until later in life often provided that creative spark she so often used to encourage the next generation. Maybe that's why I'm a writer today. Of course, she never tried to dictate a career path for any of those she raised or mentored, she just encouraged us to make smart choices.

And that's what's at the heart of this book—making smart, conscious, deliberate choices. You'll also meet dynamic women making bold moves of their own. What happens when we stop taking for granted that inner drive so unique to us? What happens when we explore it, understand it and then really, truly work it? Our life's work doesn't just enrich and fulfill us, but begins to make a bigger and bigger difference to others. It starts with a mindset. A mindset becomes a mantra. A mantra becomes a mission. A mission becomes a ministry, in that others join in and are uplifted by it. And what results when we work together to make positive change is often termed a miracle. The authors of this book challenge us to dream bigger dreams and then trust that inner force to make them happen. Are you ready?

Claire McIntosh is an award-winning writer and editor. At ESSENCE, she divides her time between writing and editing. She edits feature stories, columns and other sections. She also writes articles on personal growth, relationships and personal finance. McIntosh and her family reside in Brooklyn.

Introduction

For Black women, achieving professional success sometimes seems like an impossible mountain to climb. But it doesn't have to be, **IF** you have the right attitude **AND** the right climbing tools. In *Work it, Girl! The Black Woman's Guide to Professional Success*, you'll get just that. As a Black woman, you will realize that you **DO** have the strength to succeed.

This guide will keep it real by acknowledging the hundreds of 'justifications' we use to stay stuck where we are, but it will also debunk the myths of career choice (or lack thereof). It will recognize that we all have limitations, yet it will present 'doable' work options for Sisters who think there are none. Finally, it will not preach to the choir, but instead describe practical steps you can take to get where you want to be—even if you are not yet sure where that is!

When frustration about your professional standing makes you want to sing the words of a classic gospel song: "You don't have to move the mountain, but give me the strength to climb," you'll love reading about the experiences of incredible Sisters who not only found their strength to climb, but who also enjoyed the ascent. We know we can't move the mountains, but we want to prepare you for a wonderful climb. So, let's *work it, girl!*

Is the question "How do I work it?" The answer can be found in the ten chapters of this book. Designed to be informative and inspirational, *Work It, Girl! The Black Woman's Guide to Professional Success*, empowers you to enjoy a great career. First, you will be introduced to the "*Work it, Girl!* concept"- *using your talents, skills and abilities to get what you want!* Then, in ten informative, instructional and entertaining chapters, you will get a blueprint to your success, regardless of where you are professionally, or where you want to go.

Each chapter will open with an inspirational quote from a famous, successful Black woman. Then, with the fun of talking to your favorite girlfriend, but the tough love of your favorite mentor, it will discuss specific *Work it, Girl!* concepts from which every reader will benefit. You'll explore the obstacles you have encountered or will encounter and get expert advice on turning them into opportunities. Throughout the chapters, you'll also meet real life women to whom you can relate as well as read profiles of Sisters who are working it on a national level. Their stories will show you that your ups and downs are similar to those of many other Black women and motivate you to continue the climb.

But desire and motivation aren't enough to succeed, you also need tools. So, every chapter will include a *Work it, Girl!* **To-Do List** with very practical steps you can take to implement our suggestions and **Action Planner** worksheets that will help you strategize your own next steps.

Finally, at the end of the book, we provide **"The Write Tools"** section, designed to show you how to *work it* the "write" way with samples and advice! The *Work It, Girl!* **Style Profile** provides relevant insight on dressing the part of success and is sure to stand the test of time.

CHAPTER 1
10 Good Choices You Can Make for Professional Success

"You did what you knew how to do. When you knew better, you did better."
– Maya Angelou (writer/poet)

What exactly is "working it?" By our definition, it is when you make the choice to use your talents, skills and abilities to get what you want. In effect, you work situations to your advantage to yield positive results. Your decision to read this book demonstrates that you are interested in "working it" to achieve success in your professional life and we assure you that you made a great choice! Now, it's time to make some more.

Choices…Choices…Choices…

Each day we make personal and professional choices that can impact our lives for years to come. Therefore, it is important for you to attempt to make these choices good ones, as you embark on your quest for career success. By "good" choices, we mean ones that will get you where you want to be, ones that you will gladly own and ones that you truly believe will make you happy. JaQuitta Williams, a thirty-something Atlanta-based television news anchor, reporter and host, shares her journey of good choices with us:

"As a broadcast journalist, my career has presented more choices than the average professional woman's, like for what TV station do I want to work? In what market do I want to work? What role do I want to take? Do I want to be an anchor, a reporter, or a little bit of both? Or, what about hosting a show?

"More than ten years ago I *chose* to move up from market to market, starting with Augusta, Georgia, my hometown. I made the choice to start out at home because I needed a family base, and their support. After all, this is a tough business. When I was ready, I branched out to Tennessee, North Carolina, Missouri, and now here to Atlanta, Georgia. I'm back in my home state.

"I came here because, frankly, I grew weary of moving and being so far away from home. I was NOT a fan of the Midwest, so I decided to leave Missouri after two years. I told my agent that he could continue to look for television work for me in Atlanta and I would look for work outside of the business. Yes, I was considering a career change. But, as God would have it, NOT LUCK, I landed as a freelancer at WSB-TV (ABC) in Atlanta. I believe God puts you where he wants you to be. The freelancing quickly turned into full-time work and I am currently the weekend anchor and reporter.

"I also *chose* to start at the bottom and work my way up through the ranks. I worked as teleprompter, studio camera operator, associate producer and eventually producer for the morning show. I later became producer/reporter then reporter/anchor and worked my way up to a 5 o'clock anchor slot in less than four years. This is NOT how every woman in this business moves up and from market to market, but this way was mine and I am happy with it.

"I eventually want to have a family, but finding Mr. Right (who actually doesn't exist—nor does Ms. Right) is difficult when you're always moving. But, I do plan on staying put for a while, here in Atlanta, unless an incredible opportunity presents itself. If that happens, I may pack my bags yet again. I'll cross that bridge when I get to it. I haven't stayed anywhere for more than three and a half years, but this, too, is a choice I've made and I am happy with it. I have made the choice to be patient. When it's time, it will come. I don't worry about when, or if, I'll meet someone. I *choose* to just go, to live, and if it happens, it will happen. Life is a journey and I *choose* to consider myself to be, now and always, a work in progress. And I am happy."

Maybe you are faced with the choice of whether you want to do what it takes to get ahead in your current job. If all the people getting promoted at work are pulling 60-hour work weeks, compared to your 40, you've got to make a decision. Do you want to remain in your current position and spend more time with your family? Or, will you opt to take on a longer workday to vie for the next promotion?

Another scenario could involve pursuing employment elsewhere. Finding a new job isn't an easy task; but, being stuck in one that doesn't satisfy you is even worse. No matter how many reasons you can come up with for not being able to land the job of your dreams, there are just as many reasons why you should try. For starters, you deserve it!

Imagine for just one moment that what you did for a living didn't feel like work. That most days you look forward to going to your j-o-b, *and* you get paid for doing something that you really love. How about taking a risk to turn your hobby into a career? It could happen.

We'll start with ten good choices you can make to achieve professional success. Are you ready for the climb?

1. Acknowledge your obstacles, then move on.

Sisters, we all have valid reasons for being where we are, but we don't have to let them stop us from living our professional dream. Instead of allowing obstacles to distract you, overwhelm you, or keep you stuck where you are, use them as the first steps in your plan for action.

If you have ever said: "I want out of this job, BUT..." I don't have time to look for another one; I don't want to go back to school; I don't know where to start; or, I don't know what else I would be happy doing," it's time to turn those stumbling blocks into stepping stones by changing your perspective. Say instead, "I want out of this job SO, I am going to make time to look for another one...go back to school...contact a career counselor...do something about it!" You'll be pleasantly surprised at how a whole new outlook just might be your catalyst for change.

2. Decide what professional success means to you.

Webster's Dictionary defines success as the gaining of something desired, planned or attempted. How do you define it? Is that *something* money? Power? Respect? Personal fulfillment?

Your success is whatever YOU want it to be and the very moment that you define success in your own terms, will be the very moment that you take your first step toward achieving it.

If you want to do what you love and love what you do in the process of attaining success, take time to look at your whole self. It is critical that you conduct a thorough assessment of your needs, wants, values, and interests before you begin to climb. What's the point of the climbing to the top of the mountain if you'll end up tumbling right back down it?

3. Write down your goals and set an agenda for achieving them.

We know that there are only 24 hours in a day, always has been, always will be. But we also agree with author Diana Scharf, who once said, "Dreams are goals with deadlines." So, don't just get busy writing down all your long-term and short-term professional goals, but be ready to commit to them by determining a time frame for achieving them. After that, the rest is just a matter of time management. This may be the most difficult choice to commit to, but you'll have to find ways to incorporate your plan for success into your current way of living, period!

4. Get comfortable with networking.

If you can't stand the thought of 'working the room' or of asking a complete stranger for a job, then you have the potential to be a great networker because that is EXACTLY what networking is NOT. Networking boils down to establishing and nurturing professional relationships that may later result in your making informed career decisions or learning about job opportunities before the word hits the street. It's about professional visibility and relationships that can benefit you. Furthermore, career experts agree that networking continues to top the list as THE most valuable job search strategy.

To be an effective networker, you'll have to prepare and practice, much as you would for a job interview. Be prepared to articulate your professional interests, listen well, ask probing questions, and always ask for another referral. Most professionals understand the value of networking and will respond positively to being engaged in conversation. So, if you are still nervous about networking, don't be. It gets easier with practice—just do it!

5. Maintain a professional image at all times.

Whether or not your plan includes looking for a new job, you must always be at your professional best in your attire, job performance and how you relate to others. Everyone around you should be able to picture you at the level to which you aspire, even if they have no idea that you are working to get there. Do whatever it takes to avoid compromising situations at work like office gossip, office politics, office romance and questionable work ethics. And whatever you do, don't use your current employer's resources (time, computer, telephone, copy machine, etc.) to look for another job!

6. Find several mentors.

No (wo)man is an island, so don't stand alone in your journey to success! Your greatest professional support can come from having several mentors who can give you insight that might help you achieve your goals. As you network in different circles, observe people who are where you want to be or are significantly closer to it than you are. Determine with whom you might feel comfortable enough to approach and discuss the possibility of a mentoring relationship.

The most productive mentoring comes from those who are openly willing to provide key information that might help you strategize your career moves and deal with professional dilemmas when they arise. Don't be discouraged or take it personally when people are not interested in helping you. Move on to find someone else who will. For more information and tips about mentoring, visit www.mentoringgroup.com.

7. Subscribe to the lifelong learning concept.

Whether you want to get a job, change jobs, or keep the one you have, you should know that the only way to stay in the game is to always be at the top of yours. Savvy professionals are those who proactively seek out professional development opportunities. The good news is that this doesn't necessarily mean enrolling in a full-fledged college degree program. You can expand your horizons by taking career enhancing courses in areas like public speaking, computer programs, business etiquette and management techniques. Professional associations, local business organizations, and community colleges offer these in the form of conferences and workshops, continuing education courses, and web-based training at relatively low costs. However, if you do make the choice to pursue an associate's, bachelor's, master's or doctorate degree, map out your plan and act on it! In any case, whether you go the professional development route or the full-time collegiate route, some employers will foot the bill as long as you can demonstrate that it would be an invest-ment, and not just an expense. Or, splurge and invest in yourself!

8. Join a professional association and be an active member.

Active membership has its privileges, so get your money's worth by taking advantage of all of them. Make it a point to attend meetings, semi-nars and conferences to expand 'who you know' and 'what you know' in your field. Volunteer for committees within the association to expand 'who knows you!' Stay abreast of new developments and technologies in your current field and others you may like to pursue by reading the publi-cations that come along with your membership. In addition to articles, these publications often include announcements for opportunities to have your writing published, to attend or present at conferences, to participate in research projects, and job openings in your field.

9. Always be prepared to launch a job search.

Whether you decide to jump ship or are thrown overboard, here are some tactical moves that will keep you afloat.

1. *Don't update your resume, write a new one* to get a fresh perspective on what you have to offer an employer. Job announcements contain clues of what hiring authorities are looking for in potential candidates.

2. *Scour your performance evaluations and training records* to see whether your achievements match the job requirements and to determine whether you need additional training to land your dream job.

3. *Ask many others for input on your resume.* Ask people in the same field to make suggestions on its content and solicit other people to proof documents for typographical errors.

4. *Test the waters.* If you feel comfortable with the idea, send out a few resumes to gauge the effectiveness of it and to determine how prepared you are for the job search. Don't overdo it though, an employer who finds out that you were not seriously looking for work may not request an interview with you the next time you apply for a position there.

10. Use the Internet for all it is worth.

Yes, there are millions of jobs on the Internet, but there are millions of people applying for them, too. Don't let that discourage you though, the information superhighway has a lot more to offer. *Want to become more familiar with a potential career?* Check out sites like the U.S. Bureau of Labor Statistics' Occupational Outlook Handbook (www.bls.gov/oco) to get excellent overviews of entire careers fields and specific jobs within them, including employment trends, earning potential and job requirements for entry and advancement. *Need job search or career change advice?* You'll find plenty of articles that contain up-to-date information on the job market, resume writing and interviewing techniques at sites like The Black Collegian Online (www.blackcollegian.com); the Career Center at IMDiversity.com; at Monster.com and on careerbuilder.com. *Want to gain better insight on a potential employer?* Comb their web site to find networking contacts, tailor your resume and prepare for job interviews. You'll find their job openings, annual report, press releases and even information about compensation and benefits packages. *If you feel the need to connect with other job hunters, colleagues or people in your targeted field*, online discussions, newsgroups, and message boards make it easy to exchange information with them.

Finally, once you are prepared to compete for job openings, check out some of the major ones cited earlier and sites like hotjobs.com and jobtrak.com. Niche sites, which cater to specific professions, ethnic groups or employment categories, may also prove beneficial. Some to try are JobAccess.org, which caters to persons with disabilities; the National Black MBA Association (nbmbaa.org) and freetimejobs.com for freelance and short-term jobs.

The Internet can be a great tool, if you know what you want from it. Therefore, we suggest you consult books on efficient use of the Internet and books that contain categorized directories of web sites. Do this in an efficient way so that you don't spend hours on end working the 'Net', instead of networking!

WORK IT, GIRL! TO-DO LIST

✔ **Know thyself.** Contact the HR department at work, the career center at your alma mater, or the state employment office to find career counselors or employment specialists who are trained to administer formal assessment instruments. Ask about the Strong Interest Inventory, the Myers-Briggs (personality) Type Indicator (MBTI) or the Career Beliefs Inventory. If this doesn't pan out, head to the bookstore or library and peruse *What Color is Your Parachute?* by Richard Bolles; *Do What You Are* by Paul D. Tieger and Barbara Barron-Tieger; or *I Could Do Anything If I Only Knew What It Was* by Barbara Sher.

✔ **Plan your next move.** Start with your most immediate goal and pick a date by which you'd like to achieve it. Then, make a list of all the tasks involved and write them in pencil on a calendar. Breaking down the process into manageable parts gives you control to make adjustments as needed and keeps you motivated because each time you accomplish something, no matter how big or small, you experience a taste of success. Once you accomplish that goal, then move on to planning your tasks for the next. Remember, if you plan one goal at a time and keep it simple, you'll stick to it!

✔ **Prepare to network.** Make a list of any groups to which you belong. Include a sorority, alumni association, athletic team, church group and your children's teams and activities. Identify people in those groups with whom you would feel comfortable approaching to ask for career-based referrals. Call them or plan to approach them the next time the opportunity arises. Write down what you will say and practice it ahead of time.

10 Good Choices You Can Make for Professional Success

It's time to ask yourself the hard question. What is your definition of success?

Debt free, with plenty invested to retire at a youthful age, active in my church, and be a blessing to others.

Make a list of 5 goals you would like to achieve in your professional life.

1) _Reach 6 figures in my profession. (Sales)_
2) _Make an extra $50K + per year in my MLM bus._
3) _Open a natural nail shop_
4) _Be the manager of my son dueing his NFL years_
5) _Write a successful book._

(_The_ Work It, Girl! To-Do _List at the end of Chapter One provides additional goal setting suggestions._)

Make a list of five people in your support group that can help you reach your goals. This list will also be a great tool for networking and identifying potential mentors.

Name	How can this person assist me?
1) _Ron LeBeau_	_Succeed goal of 6 figures_
2) _Dave & Lisa Telover_	_Make 50K per year from MLM_
3) _Charlotte Summer_	_Open Natural Nail shop._
4) _Cherie Bell_	_Managing Jordan in NFL_
5) _Debora Gregory_	_Writing Successful book._

Write down three excuses that you are making in your quest for professional success.

1) _Fear_

2) _Time_

3) _Knowledge_

Now think about every excuse you've listed and write down ways to overcome these stumbling blocks and obstacles. Believe that you can succeed. Choose to think positive and take action.

Self-Talk + Action to Kill the Fear, Plan daily. Start to read, research how goals will be achieved.

Networking:
Make a list of any groups to which you belong and identify those people within those groups who can help you reach your career goals.

Group: **Resource Person(s):**

1) _HBA_   _Apt. Mgrs to work agreements with_

2) _UR Association_   _Miller + TePoller for bus. growth_

3) _WIN Group_   _Brenda + Autumn w/NAIL shop development._

Create and write down your own professional affirmation or mantra:

I Can; I will; I do! (Phil. 4:13)

WORK IT, GIRL! PROFILE OF MARIA DOWD

Maria Dowd's choice to start African American Women on Tour (AAWOT) in 1991 greatly impacted the lives of Black women. Held in over 40 U.S. cities, the Caribbean and France over the course of 13 years, AAWOT heralded the holistic (body, mind and spirit) approach to wellness. In 2003 Dowd made the choice to end the empowerment series. She remains an empowering source for women with her series of books that started with the debut of her first title, *Journey to Empowerment*. She is also one of the top grossing sales consultants for Warm Spirit, a company that provides beauty and self-care products. She has amassed a national following and the authors of *Work It, Girl!* caught up with this busy entrepreneur to get her take on choices.

Six Questions for Maria Dowd:

1) **WIG**: How did you make the choice to start African American Women on Tour (AAWOT) in 1991?

Maria Dowd: *I simply sensed the need for an empowerment conference for Black women, something not tied to a religion, profession or sorority, where women could come and let their hair "out" and gain greater insight and knowledge on why and how to live a more joyful, balanced life.*

2) **WIG**: How difficult was it for you to make the **choice** to end the women's conference series in 2003?

Maria Dowd: *It wasn't difficult at all...by that time. AAWOT's cycle was complete, and I was ready to move on to other things that fed me...and with less work and stress.*

3) WIG: What do you believe are the best and worst **choices** you've made in your career?

Maria Dowd: *The best choice was joining the Warm Spirit community as a wellness and self-care consultant. It's an environment that allows me to leverage the entrepreneurial spirit of many, rather than reliance on just myself. It represents cooperative economics, financial freedom and the soul of Black women.*

The worst choice was continuing African American Women on Tour for about three years longer than I should have. I totally ignored all indicators that the conference would downturn, as the cycle of all things do. Corporations were downsizing left and right, and pulling back on the very budgets that financed AAWOT.

4) WIG: How has your **choice** to join Warm Spirit impacted your life journey?

Maria Dowd: *In many amazing ways. I've developed my selling, coaching and public speaking skills tremendously. I have an entire community of people willing and able to support me in every way that I need, and vice versa. I don't feel like I'm out there all by myself trying to figure out my next moves. And, earning residual and passive income is the greatest. As I sashay into my fifties, I want that dance to be with ease, grace and financial freedom.*

5) WIG: What advice can you give to our readers about making good **choices**?

Maria Dowd: *Listen to your intuition. And, be willing to pay for expert advice in those areas where you could use the help or support. Discover your soul's purpose; then work your magic.*

6) WIG: What, in your opinion, is the difference between "working" and "working it?"

Maria Dowd: *Very cool question. I literally just used the term "working it" today. "Working" suggests not having control of your destiny. "Working it" suggests confidence and clarity…knowing that you are in your element, "doing you" and manifesting your dreams.*

For more information on Maria Dowd visit her online at www.MariaDowd.biz.

CHAPTER 2
Having a Career that You Are Passionate About

"I believe you're here to live your life with a passion. Otherwise you're just traveling through the world blindly—and there's no point to that."
–Oprah Winfrey (media superwoman, philanthropist)

Most of us have been told, at some point, that if we follow our hearts and do what we love, then the money will follow. Some of us, like Tyna Andrews, a Los Angeles-based choreographer and certified natural health professional who has a lifetime of memories about her passion, did just that. Later in life she reaped the riches, literally and figuratively.

"All my life I have been involved in some aspect of dance. My grand-father always said I was born moving. Whenever I hear a beautiful song I immediately want to create the movement to it because seeing the music makes beautiful memories," she said.

Tyna still remembers performing in little homemade productions with her cousins at five years old. She was the first Black cheerleader captain at J.E.B. Stuart High School in Falls Church, Virginia. She minored in dance and business while working toward a bachelor's degree in psychology, and she directed Howard University's Ooh La La Dancers while attending graduate school to earn a degree in exercise physiology.

Since 1991 when Tyna completed her master's degree, she has amassed an impressive list of credentials. They include working on the early stages of the movie "What's Love Got To Do with It?" with the same choreographer who worked on Michael Jackson's "Thriller," coordinating productions at Disneyland Resort in California, and being on staff at the Amazing Grace Conservatory for the past ten years. Her television projects include being a talent executive for "BET Live" and for "Oh Drama!" Most recently, Tyna has found a way to merge her exercise physiology education with dance movement into the healing arena by providing these services to corporate and community clientele. And although she is extremely proud of the recognition she has received for her work, Tyna will be quick to tell you that nothing beats the feeling of *working it* when you love what you do. *"I feel like I am doing what I was born to do. It just feels right, and I know it's a blessing. Sometimes I say to myself, 'Wow! I get paid to do this!'"*

Unfortunately, there are still far too few of us who believe 'this can happen to me' and therefore we ignore the advice to 'do what you love'. Then, before we know it, it seems like it is too late, and we are unwilling or unable to venture out and follow our hearts. The good news is that we, the authors, are among many experts who believe that it is NEVER too late to pursue your passion!

Discovering Your Passion

Sometimes discovering your passion doesn't progress as naturally as it did with Tyna, but that doesn't mean you can't make it happen! If you are ready to live your passion, and are willing to do what it takes to figure out what it is, then let's *work it!*

The first step in uncovering your passion is to realize that no one is ever going to be able to tell you what will make you happy; it's all up to you to take a personal journey of self-assessment. Simply put, self-assessment is a process of determining who you are and what you want. With respect to your career management, it's the road to determining what will bring you career satisfaction. There are many formal, standardized self-assessment tools available to measure your skills, interests, personality types, work, values, etc., and it is always advisable to partner with a career counselor to get the greatest benefits from such instruments, including clearly understanding each tool's purpose, having realistic expectations for using it, and interpreting the results.

But as the saying goes, never put off until tomorrow what you can do today. Below you will find an introductory (and hopefully fun) writing exercise to start you thinking about what's *really* your passion. As you complete it, don't skip over any of the questions in haste to find the answer. The answer is in the process. Here are a few stipulations before you get started.

Select a quiet writing area where you will not be interrupted.

Be prepared to spend a minimum of 15 minutes answering each question.

Don't be afraid to think back into your childhood, many answers are likely to be found there.

Don't feel obligated to answer all the questions in order, or in one sitting. In fact, you'll probably do much better if you answer them over several sittings.

Don't think about what you are writing, or worry about correctness, just write.

Don't rush. If you get on a roll with a particular question, don't stop until you have written all that comes to mind. Trust us, when you are on the way to discovering your passion, you'll be fueled by the excitement, so take advantage of the momentum! The more you write down in your responses, the closer you'll be to discovering your dream job or career.

After you have answered *all* the questions, complete Part II. If you get so excited about discovering yourself that you answer all the questions on the same day, DO NOT complete Part II until at least three days later.

Ready? Set? Write!
Part I

1. If you inherited or won a couple of cool millions would you or would you not still get up and go to a j-o-b every day? Would you get up and go to your current j-o-b?

2. If money wasn't an issue, how would you spend your days? Why?

3. What kinds of things are you doing when time seems to fly?

4. What are you doing when you feel most productive?

5. What are you doing when you feel happiest?

6. What are your talents, strengths, and abilities?

7. How do you escape feeling overwhelmed at work or home?

8. What did you always think you wanted to be when you grew up? Why did you or did you not become that?

9. What in your life *really matters most*?

Part II

Now that you have answered all the questions, go back and read through your responses. As you do so, write down your reactions on a separate sheet of paper or anything that comes to mind while reading what you wrote. Jot down any patterns you notice. What connections can you make between the things you love to do and potentially meaningful careers? Which of those careers could potentially be your passion?

This beginning of self-assessment will not only increase your understanding of who you are and what makes you tick—a vital part in figuring out your passion—but it will also uncover what types of jobs will make good use of your passion AND strengths. In these answers, and your evaluation of them, is where you are likely to find your niche and your true ability to *work it*.

Always remember that self-assessment is the first step in a *continuous* process of career planning and management. Throughout your professional life, you *will* change, and thus, periodic re-evaluation is a must.

Also, remember what we said earlier, no one is ever going to be able to tell you what will make you happy. But those who *know* you can tell you what they think you are good at doing. So don't be afraid to ask around about what others see as your "hidden talents."

Work it, Girl! Live Your Dream

Have you ever been asked by others to do something for which you have a special talent? Have you ever been offered money just for putting to use a particular skill, something you simply like to do? Do people think you are an expert in some area? Do you regularly get compliments about an ability that others recognize in you? If you can answer 'yes' to any of these questions, then you may have just figured out (or confirmed) your passion! Now what?

It's ironic that passion is described by *Webster's Collegiate Thesaurus* as an intense, high-wrought emotion that compels [one] to action, because when it comes to pursuing one's *career* passion, far too few people are so compelled to act. Instead, they stay in jobs for which they don't have much interest, let alone enthusiasm. Even worse, they spend

27

so much time and energy at unfulfilling jobs, that pursuing their passion outside of the workplace through volunteering or as a hobby isn't even possible. Sound familiar? If you haven't made a move toward pursuing something new, what's stopping you?

DO SOME-thing, ANY-thing. Teach. Write. Volunteer. Study. Read. Whatever it takes to steadily infuse that passion into your life and generate some excitement.

Lila Johnson is a woman who infused her passion into her career. The medical professional has combined her medical training and love for travel into a very exciting and rewarding career. In about eight years, she has traveled to 17 different nursing assignments, each of them lasting from three to six months. Here is how she did it:

After having been an RN in several medical and surgical hospital units, Lila Johnson became bored with her work and began to look for another job. While reading a magazine she came across an ad for travel nursing and couldn't resist calling the telephone number listed to find out more information. After all, she had always LOVED to travel. Unfortunately, she discovered that she did not have the one year of experience the job required. But, that small item only delayed Lila's living her dream, it did not prevent her from living it. One year later, Lila contacted that company again to apply for the travel nursing job. And the rest, as they say, is history. Lila is starting her seventh year as a travel nurse and has no plans to settle down anytime soon. In fact, this traveling nurse likens herself to Mary Poppins: *"I come in to help the hospital staff over their hump and when it is time to go, I say goodbye and move on. That was a good experience,"* she said, *"but I just love to travel, so I got back on the road."*

For Lila, traveling just feels natural. *"As a child, my mom wanted us to know there was more to life than Kansas City, so every summer we would take a vacation. As an adult, I started treating myself to a birthday trip to a different place every year. I've gone to San Diego, Las Vegas, a cruise to Cozumel, the Florida Keys and London. Travel nursing feeds my need to travel and pays the bills. Maybe I enjoy it so much because I never felt I belonged in any one spot, but instead felt like I belonged everywhere!"*

To many of us, this all might sound too good to be true, but the simple fact of the matter is that the people who are happiest about their work are those who are doing what they love. And, in light of recent world events, it's time for us to be more cognizant of what's important in our lives and to re-evaluate the role our career plays in our overall happiness.

Sharlene, a program manager for treatment foster care in Maryland followed what she describes as a "calling" in her path to career happiness.

"I developed a desire to help people with their problems ever since I was little girl. For some reason people would feel comfortable telling me their problems. When I went to Morgan State University from 1991 to 1995, I found out that the ability that I had was called social work," said Sharlene Allen.

"Upon graduating, I knew I wanted to do therapy, so I went to Smith College School for Social Work and earned a master's degree in clinical social work by the time I was 23 years old. Helping people with their problems became a passion for me when I realized that I could have been any one of the teenagers or adults that I have served. I had also struggled with depression and low self-worth; and through my relationship with God I overcame those issues that once oppressed me. There are a whole lot of people out there who struggle with some issue or another and often feel that there is no way out. I am the person to help them find hope and that way out.

"What God did for me, I have a desire to do for others through His guidance. Because of my personal experiences, I started a ministry called W.O.R.D. (Walk Obediently and Receive Deliverance) in September 2001. As a result of my spiritual walk with God, He saw fit to have me ordained as a minister at the age of 28, in June 2002. I truly enjoyed being a mental health worker in a poor section in Baltimore, with patients who

struggle with mental illness. I enjoyed it, because it falls in line with what I have discovered to be my purpose in life."

When you are living your passion it shows. Because of her obvious excitement for her work, Sharlene has been invited to share her passion outside of her regular job, and to her, it just doesn't feel like work.

"I have had the opportunity to facilitate workshops on depression and low self-esteem in local churches, speak at a school assembly after 9/11, provide therapy for children and adolescents at the church I attend, and most recently, be the main speaker at a church service in Jamaica.

The greatest benefit of having a career that you are passionate about is that you are able to deliver service from the core of your being, because that is what you were purposed to do."

While engaging in the self-assessment aspect of finding your passion, you must also evaluate what you are currently doing to determine whether it fits or will fit into your dreams. We urge you not to simply discover your passion, but step out there and live it because you *can* have it all!

WORK IT, GIRL! TO-DO LIST

✔ **Stop making excuses:** Lack of Skills? Skills can be learned. Once you find your passion, you'll be motivated to acquire the skills and the will to succeed, simply because you love what you're doing. Lack of Education? Education, like skills, can be acquired. With careful research and career exploration, you will find that acquiring education doesn't always have to mean enrolling in a full degree program. Community college classes, online courses, and professional development training are all avenues to increasing your ability to *work it*. Afraid to change jobs or careers? On average, a person will have three careers across her life span and even more jobs than that. So, it's ok if you are not happy in this job or career, but now is the time to find a new one. Believe that you have to be among the best to profit from working at your passion? The real deal is that you must *do* your best, not *be* the best.

✔ **Create a plan for passion:** No matter how difficult it seems to incorporate what you love to do into your crazy, hectic life, make room for your passion. Write a list of actions you can take to further your quest for doing what you love and schedule time to do it. For example, you can begin by scheduling 15 minutes a day to accomplish any of the following items. Answer the self-assessment questions from this chapter, review them and record your thoughts. Read books, trade magazines, or web sites that cater to those who share your interests.

✔ **Get involved in your passion:** Reading about what you love to do is a great way to start the ball rolling, but getting personally involved will be considerably more fulfilling. Schedule time to seek volunteer opportunities and then commit to doing them. Whether you volunteer weekly or monthly, you could gain experience and confidence to help you change your job or career. Write, speak, or teach what you love to do. Almost nothing will be more satisfying than enabling others to experience the passion you share. Finally, conducting informational interviews with people who do what you love, could generate just the level of motivation you need to propel you into action. Who knows? You might not only discover your passion, but you may also discover your life's purpose.

Having a Career that You Are Passionate About

Record your answer to the burning question, "What are you passionate about professionally?"

Teaching, coaching, mentoring, empowering others.

Now that you've identified your passion, it's time to take action!
List five ways that you can pursue your passion on a regular basis. Place a star next to the three items you are ready to implement immediately.

1) _Thru my business_ ★
2) _On my Job_ ★
3) _In my church_
4) _Thru my pack this friends_ ★
5) _Volunteering_

Who is one person that you think personifies passion in their career endeavors:

Joel Osteen

Describe how that person demonstrates his or her passion:

You can tell in his ministry rather it is him speaking, his books, the daily devotion emails that he is passionate leading people to Christ & helping achieve beyond their expectations

Use them as examples to you!

Learn and repeat this mantra:

"Pursuing my professional passion is a gift I pledge to give to myself today, tomorrow, and always!"

Honor a binding contract with yourself:

I, _Shalonda_, will not make excuses. I will nurture my plan for passion. I will be actively engaged in the pursuit of my goals by immediately engaging in the three items by which I placed a star (above).

Shalonda Haynes
Signature

_8/17/2013_
Date

WORK IT, GIRL! PROFILE OF LORRAINE MORRIS COLE AND PAMELA M. MCBRIDE

We, Lorraine Morris Cole and Pamela M. McBride, the authors of *Work It, Girl!* feel that this is the perfect time to introduce ourselves to you, our readers. Why this chapter? Because you wouldn't be reading these words right now if we did not have such a strong *passion* for and unwavering dedication to this project. This book idea was conceived in July of 2002 and we have traveled a long road to bring it to life. We, my Sisters, have a testimony that is best summarized in these words, "never give up on your dream." What you are holding in your hands, this book, is the embodiment of our collaborative dream. This chapter is all about passion and we hope this Q & A with us will provide an insightful profile of our journey to this place in our lives and empower you to pursue your passion.

Three Questions for Lorraine Morris Cole:

1) When did you discover that writing was your passion?

Lorraine Morris Cole: *I think my most vivid memories of my discovery of my love for writing was in the fifth grade. I won an essay contest at Downer Elementary. I remember getting special recognition and a letter from the lieutenant governor of South Carolina. I was so proud of that accomplishment and so happy to see how proud my mother, father and sister were of me. Although I was writing before that time, that accomplishment was my catalyst to really pursue my love for writing. I think it was the answer "yes," to the question in my young mind of whether or not I was a writer. It was a wonderful revelation that opened up a whole new realm of possibilities for me. It was the discovery of a lifetime!*

2) Why is it important for women to pursue whatever it is that they are passionate about?

Lorraine Morris Cole: *I not only think it is important, I think it is crucial to self-satisfaction. It doesn't matter if you pursue your passion on a big or small scale; it's the act of honoring yourself that is important. The woman who pursues her passion for fitness by simply working out at a gym is no less successful than the woman who pursues the same passion and becomes a nationally known fitness guru. They are both winners because they pursued something that they are passionate about in life. I'm proud to say that I am one of Oprah's biggest fans and it's not only because of what she has accomplished; it's because of her "live your best life" philosophy. Women are the classic care-givers and in that giving often don't think they can carve out the time or energy for things that bring them joy. I present workshops and seminars for women throughout the year and my advice is always, you don't have to neglect yourself in your quest to be of service to others. In fact, being good to yourself helps you to be better to others.*

3) Why are you passionate about the book *Work It, Girl!* and empowering Black women?

Lorraine Morris Cole: *From the time we conceptualized this idea we embraced it with a passion. It is that passion that helped us travel the long road to publication. We had people in the publishing industry tell us that "Black women don't need specialized advice." We got rejected by agents and publishers who didn't share our vision of a career guide designed to empower Black women. Yet, like Shirley Chisholm, we decided to be "unbought and unbossed," and stayed true to our vision for this book. Ultimately and happily, we landed at Parker Publishing; a publishing house that shares our vision for Black literature.*

My desire to empower Black women is a result of the wonderful women who have, in some way, enriched my life. I have been empowered by my grandmothers, my mother, sisters, aunts, cousins, teachers, friends, coworkers, sorority sisters—there are just too many to name them all! Yet the impact of my Sister circle inspired me to start book clubs, conduct seminars and workshops, and write articles with the Black woman in mind. My efforts to empower Black women are my small way of giving back for all the great things that they have given me.

Three Questions for Pamela M. McBride:

1) When did you discover that writing was your passion?

Pamela M. McBride: *I didn't discover my passion for writing until I was in my late twenties, but I discovered my love of words long before then. As a child I was an avid reader. In fact, I can remember winning a t-shirt with* Bookworm *written across it because I read more books than any other second grader in my school. I vividly recall working in my elementary school library just to get more time to read. Since I always read fiction back then, I wished I could write it. Unfortunately, I never thought I was creative enough to do it well. So, I just continued reading and reading until I realized much later that I could write nonfiction in a creative way. Then, a writer was "born". As a career counselor I was passionate about helping others make good choices about their professional lives. I knew I was creative when it came to conducting my workshops, seminars, and counseling sessions because my students and clients told me so. When a co-worker showed an article of hers that had been published, my thoughts were: I can do that. She taught me how to write a query letter and from that point on, I wrote article, after article, after article, combining my professional expertise as a career counselor and my creativity with the written (nonfiction) word. I somehow knew that one day I would write a book.*

2) Why is it important for women to pursue whatever it is that they are passionate about?

Pamela M. McBride: *When a woman is passionate about something, it propels her forward in that area and often leads to new experiences as well. Besides, if it is a true passion, it is probably more difficult to resist the passion than to go with the flow of pursuing it. For three very recent years I allowed a hectic work life to come between me and my writing. Honestly, I just couldn't fathom having the time or energy to do it. I was exhausted and saw no end in sight. Yet, when God placed the opportunity to write this book right back in my lap, I not only found the time to do it, but as much as it consumed nearly all of the few sleep hours I had, it* *somehow energized me. It brought a pleasure that I truly missed right back into my life. And it made a difference! Even when I only got two hours of sleep, I felt energized. Don't get me wrong, there were some challenges to my endurance in the process, but it just didn't matter because I was doing something to feed my soul. I believe it is important for all women to figure out what passion will re-energize them because as giving creatures, we tend to give to others and not to ourselves. My hope is that every reader gives herself the gift of finding and pursuing her passion so she will be more energized for everything else in her life. And then, I hope she spreads the word!*

3) Why are you passionate about the book *Work It, Girl!* and empowering Black women?

Pamela M. McBride: *I am passionate about the book because I believe in every word of it! I believe in the power of empowering women through their own choices and their own definition of success. I believe that the TO-DO Lists and Action Planners will empower our Sisters to immediately implement every idea they think is a good one, making a difference for themselves and for others around them. I believe in the feelings of security and support brought on by having a close group of Sister–friends and we want each of our readers to feel as though the women we have included in our work of passion are part of their own Sister circle. Black women are our foundation of life. I want to do my part to contribute to our legacy.*

CHAPTER 3
You Can Have It All

"Believe in yourself and your abilities. There are lots of folks who'll tell you 'It can't be done'."
—Jasmine Guy (star of stage and screen, author, wife and mother)

Janet Lovejoy is CEO of her own computer consulting firm. She works 6-8 hour days, no evening or weekend work. She absolutely never brings work home. The money is great. Her two children are perfect angels. The Supermom doesn't miss a ballet recital or soccer game. The relationship that she has with her husband of eight years is truly what romance novels are made of; they have never had a moment of conflict. Her many organizations and activities fit perfectly into her schedule. She always has quality time for herself, her children and her husband. When she looks in the mirror she's a perfect size 8, her skin is a flawless tawny color and her hair is stunning.

If you believe that we've also got some swampland in Florida to sell you after you finish reading this book! Janet Lovejoy is not a real person. This case study is fiction. Yet, many of us imagine perfection. We're not happy because we are chasing an elusive fairytale.

Some women fall victim to their imaginations when they can identify successful women who they feel "have it all." They picture these kinds of women in blissful states of managing their personal and professional lives. What they really see, however, is not perfection, but great examples of women who are "working it"—using their talents, skills and abilities to get what they want. You, too, can *work it*. You can effectively balance your world. You *can* have it all!

How do women define having it all? It depends on whom you ask. While writing *Work It, Girl!* we talked with many Sisters and weren't shocked to find that what "having it all" means to a career woman who is 23 and single can be very different from what it means to a 30- or 40-year-old woman who is married with children. The single women, in some cases, were more focused on balancing careers and social lives. Many of the married mothers, on the other hand, expressed their needs to be on top of their game as a professional, a wife and a mother—as expressed in the now famous commercial lyrics, "I can bring home the bacon. Fry it up in the pan. And never, never, let you forget you're a man. Cause I'm a woman!"

If your definition of having it all is successfully balancing your career, motherhood and being a wife, we've got great news for you. It *can* be done. But, sometimes you have to "think outside of the box." According to an article in *Ebony* magazine, Candace Matthews did just that when she was offered the presidency of SoftSheen-Carson, one of the world's leaders in the ethnic hair and beauty products industry. The act of "thinking outside the box" resulted in her husband, Bruce Matthews, becoming a stay-at-home dad or househusband. How has that benefited her in her quest to be a great corporate president, mother, and wife? Joy Bennett Kinnon who authored the article states, "knowing that home is taken care of frees Matthews to fulfill her many responsibilities."

In Chapter One, we introduced to you a TV news anchorwoman, JaQuitta Williams. The single, thirty-something media personality shared an interesting laundry list of what "having it all" means to her:

"Having it all, for me, is not just one thing. It's numerous things that are all simple. It means: living in a city I'm happy with; being close to family, but not in their back yards; having friends who are close; traveling from time to time for a getaway; taking every day as it comes; knowing that life is short and living in the moment; a visit, dinner, movie, and good conversation with a friend; knowing that I'm loved unconditionally; a long bubble bath; a glass of wine, quiet, good relaxing music and candle-light; good health; my family still being here to share in my successes and failures; having money to get what I want, for myself and my family (within

reason); and, I think a mate helps that picture, but DOES NOT complete it."

Djuanna Brockington wants to have her cake and eat it too. And why shouldn't she? After all, as a Black professional and single mother of a small child, she has worked to pay for it, shopped for its ingredients and baked it, too! The problem is that Djuanna's notion of having it all means being all things to the people in her life and doing all of it to perfection. Quite obviously, this thinking is causing her to bite off more than she can chew. No wonder she sometimes feels too "full" to function properly.

"I want my home life to run smoothly—my child to be happy, my house to be clean, and I want to be able to relax and enjoy personal time. At work, I would like to always be on top of my game—with a clear desk, an empty In Box and all my obligations met efficiently and accurately," said the social services program administrator who aspires to become an agency director.

Sound familiar? Then you should realize, like Djuanna finally has, that Superwoman is a myth and that these stressors are self-induced.

"My child could care less if the house is immaculate, and my boss understands that with the nature of our business, it is very difficult to always be on top of the paperwork because our days are often very unpredictable. But, I still want order and I have to remind myself that the world is not resting on my shoulders, so get over it."

Get over it? Absolutely! Getting caught up in The Superwoman Syndrome can rob you of the opportunities it takes to climb toward professional success. Somehow, we have been conditioned to think that the more we do, the more successful we will be. However, that may not ring true when it comes to success at work. If you feel frazzled and overworked while on-the-job, you probably appear so, too. Consequently, co-workers are less likely to involve you in any "extra" work for fear of being the straw that breaks the camel's back. Without even realizing it, you could be deemed unreliable and may not be considered for that time-consuming, yet plum, assignment.

Losing the opportunity to do such "extra" work might mean losing out on opportunities for future raises, promotions and professional recognition, not to mention that if possible layoffs ever come into play, you could be setting yourself up for becoming an unemployment statistic.

The Superwoman Syndrome will also drain you of the strength it takes to make the professional climb. If you are thinking about home at work and work at home, then it will seem like you not only have two full-time jobs, but that you are working both of them simultaneously…a sure way to become completely overwhelmed, overworked and unsatisfied. How long do you think you'll last and how far will you get under those conditions? A good strategy is to adopt the attitude that if what you have at home is a true emergency you'll take time off to handle it. The alternative of coming to work and not performing or making costly mistakes could spell disaster.

We believe that the secret to finding the right work/life balance lies in the willingness to draw a clear line between home and work. We encourage you to stop thinking that the only way to *have* it all is to figure out how to *do* it all because that simply is not the case. Having it all requires understanding the difference between doing it all and doing what matters. So, regardless of how much you love to take care of your family and how much you love being a professional woman, you must draw a clear line between the two if you want to succeed at each of them.

"I consider my home my sanctuary, and I don't let the lines become blurred," said Djuanna. *"I very seldom take work home, and when I do, I NEVER take it past my living room. I make a conscious effort to do it at the dining room table most of the time. And then I put it in the car until it's time to return to work. This gives me the peace I need in my life in order to rejuvenate for the next day."*

Djuanna definitely has the right idea. If you don't have a permanent work-at-home arrangement with your employer or you don't work for yourself, then don't make a habit of working at home, period. But, if you do find it necessary to bring work home, set boundaries for how and where you will do it.

Another boundary that needs to be in place is one that marks how you will spend your precious time. We all have a finite amount of time each day. Yet, the list of things we have to do in that time is seemingly infinite. Take control of the situation by making your 'to do' list a finite one. Instead of starting each day with an insurmountable list of things to do at work and at home, decide what things *have* to be done, do them, and let the rest go.

You can achieve this by setting aside a few minutes at the start or end of your workday and at the end of your evening at home to jot down what you'd like to accomplish the next day. Putting things down on paper will help you get focused. Making a point to cross off each item as you complete it throughout the day will help you feel more in control and more accomplished in both of your worlds. Also, be sure to consult your master schedule or calendar to safeguard against conflicts that will hinder you from performing your tasks effectively. For example, if you have a board meeting on Monday you may not want to schedule another time-consuming task on the same day.

As for simple day-to-day tasks, be careful not to let them consume too much of your time at home or at work. Plan when and for how long you will do such tasks as reading the mail, replying to e-mail and returning telephone calls and stick to it. In fact, consider using these tasks as time-out breaks from your bigger, more difficult duties. Also, keep things as organized as possible to cut down on wasting so much time looking for them when you need them.

Don't let meal times consume you either. At work, take time for yourself during your lunch hour. Exercise. Read. Plan a rendezvous with your man. Have a picnic with a Sister-friend. Get a massage or pedicure. Go to a restaurant and be served at your table. Do anything low key that you might not otherwise have the luxury to do. If you choose to eat at your desk, don't work while you do it. Set aside 20 minutes of work-free time to just relax. You might even purchase a special placemat, use silverware and listen to soothing music. If you must do personal errands at lunchtime, plan ahead by limiting these frantic lunchtime races to once a week and doing only the errands that will make another part of your day or your week less hectic.

At home, serving your family good meals during the week doesn't have to mean pot-roast cooked with potatoes and carrots, homemade rolls and fresh-squeezed lemonade unless they are leftovers from Sunday dinner! A homemade hamburger on a bun, baked French fries, any vegetable or fruit and Minute Maid lemonade is just as healthy. Campbell's Soup also provides quick, delicious and simple homemade meal ideas on their web site at www.campbellsoup.com. Many of their recipes take less than 30 minutes to prepare. Make mealtime at home a time to enjoy your family and catch up on the day's events. Commit to concentrating on your loved ones and keep discussion about work to a minimum.

Finally, remember that while trying to have your cake and eat it too, a full plate is a full plate. Sometimes, taking a little bit off your plate could make all the difference in the world in how much you enjoy what you have to do and how effective you can be when doing it. Djuanna Brockington, the South Carolina-based social services program administrator recalled when she recently discovered that fact.

"I always try to coordinate some sort of recognition for my employees' birthdays, but lately it's become more difficult for me to get it done because of an increased workload. This time, I decided to let someone else do it and what a difference! She was pleased to be chosen to carry out a function that typically is done by the supervisors and I was pleased because I was able to re-direct my focus to another project. What better way for me to encourage my employees to take ownership in the team process than giving them opportunities to assume roles outside of their normal responsibilities?"

So often, when we think about delegating, we think of projects or big things. However, sometimes it's giving away the little things that brings the greatest amount of relief. Since then, Djuanna has learned not to be afraid to delegate work-related tasks either.

"I used to feel that the work may not be as well received by superiors if it was done by someone else—that they may not have confidence in the

individual that I selected. Once I realized that there were two sides to this coin—providing my case managers with an opportunity to demonstrate their expertise and hone their skills, as well as having an assignment completed in an effective and efficient manner for upper management, it was very clear that this was a win-win situation."

If you don't have staff to whom you can delegate, then be creative in how you can use the team approach in a different way. It's a great idea to take on new projects at work for the variety and the challenge. Plus, doing so will definitely expand your knowledge and skills and make you feel good when the projects are completed. On the other hand, be reasonable about taking on too much. Instead of always volunteering to take on the entire project, volunteer for a particular part of the project so you won't get so bogged down. That way, you still have the chance to contribute while giving your co-workers the opportunity to be a part of the process as well.

Delegating works at home too. Picture in your mind a scale with each of your household chores on one side and each chore of your family members on the other side. Is it balanced? If not, imagine transferring a chore from your side of the scale to the other side and watch it even out. Now give away the weight of doing it all at home and start smiling.

When delegating household chores won't work or will cause you more stress than it's worth, don't be discouraged, hire some help. This could mean that you hire a housekeeper once or twice a month. Or, if that's too expensive, pay a teen neighbor, relative or babysitter to do light housework once a week or to take the kids to the park for three hours on Saturday morning while you get all the chores done yourself. The options are limitless so be creative and find one that works for you.

As Djuanna has learned, when all is said and done, having it all means being able to enjoy both aspects of your life without feeling guilty about either of them.

"Work and home are my yin and yang," Djuanna said. *"While I am at the office, I enjoy the organized chaos, unpredictability, and quick thinking that is needed to get through the day. When I get home, I enjoy*

the slow pace of quiet conversations and laughter with my child, and later just drinking a cup of tea and reading a book when she is in bed. If I am balanced, I can deal with any bumps in the road along the way."

Much of the strength it takes to make the professional climb will come from feeling successful at home and at work. So stop *doing* it all and start *having* it all!

Work It, Girl! To-Do List

✔ **Take back your time.** These days, even Superwoman would have a hard time keeping up with the schedules we working moms keep! After all the time and energy that goes into your home and work lives, there are still other things you struggle to fit into your schedule…bake sales, sporting events, school volunteering, religious and civic activities…at some point you have to JUST SAY NO. By no means are we saying that you should omit all these from your life. But trying to give 100% of yourself to 100% of the things out there is definitely not the answer. Figure out how much time you have or want to have to commit to these activities and don't feel guilty about what doesn't fit.

✔ **Pay yourself first…and last**. Free up your mind to be in the moment with your family and yourself. First, allot yourself 15 minutes to sit down as soon as you walk in the door. Don't read the mail, don't check the answering machine, don't start dinner and don't think about what needs to be done. Cross your feet at the ankles and put your hands behind your head. Just chill. Then, go ahead with getting done all the household chores you desire, but stop at a pre-determined time, no matter what. Make the rest of the night yours. Your goal should be to get at least one hour to yourself daily. Have the people with whom you live respect your personal time because this time can provide renewal and increase your ability to be a better caregiver and partner.

✔ **Create a support system**. When the going gets tough, even Superwoman doesn't hesitate to call on the other Super Friends and neither should you. Establish a network of other Super Moms who are willing to split the carpooling and rotate playtime. Even if it means taking on the task of coordinating the whole thing, it'll be worth it in the end. Plus, inherent in this smart move is the benefit of potentially having a built-in plan B, plan C, and plan D when unforeseen circumstances arise and you need someone who's got your back. And, it goes without saying, that you must have your Sisters' backs when they find themselves in that same tough spot.

47

You Can Have It All

List women who you think "have it all!" (This list can include people that you don't know personally.) Why do you think these women have it all?

Women

Oprah Winfrey
Michelle Obama
Adena McDonald

Why do you think she has it all?

Healthy
Position & Attitude
Family & Career

When it comes to balancing your professional and personal life, what does having it all mean to you?

Being able to still give 100% to my personal life after giving 100% to my professional including a relationship & family

Think about your regular tasks. Come up with three things that you are doing that may be contributing to a hectic lifestyle and come up with some other workable alternatives.

Example Task: I spend at least two hours preparing the evening family meal and it leaves me exhausted.

Example Alternative: Save lengthy meals for the weekend when I have more time. Many healthy meals take less time. Baking chicken and serving it with a healthy tossed salad is a great alternative. It can take less than an hour to prepare and makes great leftovers!

Current Task

Letting laundry pile-up
Think+preparing,
Putting of east tasks

Possible Alternative

Commit to it weekly
Just doing it sometimes
Complete it when needed.

What tasks are you performing, at work or home, that you can get help with?

Current Task

MDU approach (work)
Retailers (work)

Who Can Help?

Anna P.
Joan

Make a list of people to include in your Super Woman Support Group.

Mom, Sister, BFF

WORK IT, GIRL! PROFILE OF VALORIE BURTON

When Valorie Burton sold her marketing and public relations firm in 2001 she set out to pursue her passion for "helping people, women in particular, live more fulfilling lives." She is now a sought-after life coach, speaker, author and media contributor. Her collection of books, including *Why Not You? 28 days to Build Authentic Confidence,* are inspiring people who are "seeking a more purposeful path." She is living with purpose and inspiring others to do the same. The authors of *Work It, Girl!* caught up with Burton to motivate our readers in their quest to "have it all!"

Six Questions for Valorie Burton:

1) **WIG:** What advice do you have for women who suffering from what we like to call "Superwoman Syndrome" (trying to be all things to everyone)?

Valorie Burton: *Superwomen are searching for something they will never discover by doing more. What we all crave is significance— to know our lives have purpose and impact others in a meaningful way. My advice is twofold. First, get clear about your most important priority. Everything else must fall in line with the priority. And, be willing to let go of activities that no longer serve you. You have to make room for what you really want in your life. That means cutting some activities from your schedule so that there is more space to breathe.*

2) **WIG:** How can defining what's important to you enrich your life?

Valorie Burton: *Fulfillment comes when you spend your life fulfilling the purpose for which you were created. That means using your gifts, talents, passion and experiences to make a difference in the* *world. Getting clear about what's important empowers you to intentionally create the life you really want. Too many women are living by accident—accepting whatever comes along. When you define what's important to you, you begin building a foundation for living on purpose.*

3) **WIG:** In your book, *Listen to Your Life*, you state, "Most of us live our lives at just a fraction of our potential." Why do you think that is true for so many people, especially women?

Valorie Burton: *I don't think it is more true for women than men. However, I think life often gets in the way of many people's dreams. Everyday responsibilities and routines can lull you to sleep so that you don't notice that life and opportunities are passing you by. Living at your potential is a process. Once you reach your potential in one area, there's an opportunity to go higher in another area. The key is to take notice of the opportunities to maximize your potential in your personal and professional life.*

4) **WIG:** What does "having it all" mean for Valorie Burton?

Valorie Burton: *For me, "having it all" means having a loving family, a joyful relationship with my husband, being at peace, getting to do work I love every day, having the freedom to explore new and interesting opportunities, and knowing that God is pleased with how I live my life and treat others.*

5) **WIG:** What do you enjoy most about your career as a life coach, author, speaker and media contributor?

Valorie Burton: *What I enjoy most is the feedback I receive from readers, clients and audience members. I stand in awe of the courageous and bold choices people make to change their lives as a result of reading or hearing my words. I am just a vessel, and the true joy comes from being used to inspire others to experience their potential.*

6) **WIG:** What, in your opinion, is the difference between "working" and "working it?"

Valorie Burton: In my mind, if you "work it", you are working your uniqueness—the gift that you have to share with the world that enhances lives in some way. "Working" is simply about doing a job. "Working it" is about doing what you do as only you can do it—without comparing yourself to others.

Visit Valorie on the web at www.valorieburton.com.

Chapter 4

Jill of All Trades —
Mistress of Her Destiny!

"One of the sad commentaries on the way women are viewed in our society is that we have to fit in one category. I have never felt that I had to be in one category."
— Faye Wattleton (president, Center for the Advancement of Women)

Donna Maria Coles Johnson is a *"Jill of All Trades and Mistress of Her Destiny."* As a Lifestyle CEO, she believes that it's time for Black women to become the CEO of their businesses, their finances, and their lives! With careers as an attorney, author, motivational speaker and founder and president of The Handmade Beauty Network, she demonstrates that it is possible to do so.

Donna Maria became hooked on beauty products when, as a child, she accompanied her father on his weekly pharmacy visits. Years later, she became an attorney, but couldn't get away from her passion for beauty products. She began making her own cosmetics in 1993 and two years later decided to leave her lucrative corporate attorney position at a Fortune 500 company to set up her own aromatherapy and bath shop in Maryland. In 2000 she launched the Handmade Beauty Network to provide business resources to manufacturers of handmade beauty products.

Today, she proves that it is possible to create the life you love by combining what you are trained to do with what you love to do and make a living at them both. She is writing books, delivering motivational speeches, and maintaining a presence online, in magazines, and on television and radio. She also maintains a successful legal and business counseling practice which she uses to empower other women to do the same. Her message? *"If you really want to achieve a particular goal, just get out of your own way!"*

Girlfriend, you're on a roll now. The past three chapters have demonstrated quite convincingly that it is possible to have it all by holding it down at work and at home. And, in the process, you could also discover that there is more than one passion you want to pursue. Well, lucky for you, there's no need to slow your roll because there's no rule that says you have to do only one thing at a time. Sisters everywhere are proving they can manage parallel careers and they have the resumes to prove it!

In fact, some of these Sisters have not just one, but two and three careers. What's more, they excel in all of them! Some of these women include superstars, like Beyoncé Knowles. The megastar made her mark as the lead singer with the hugely successful Destiny's Child, then branched out and achieved even more as a solo artist, a successful actress in several hit movies (*The Pink Panther*, *Austin Powers*, and *Fighting Temptations*), and now, Beyoncé Knowles has reached into the world of fashion with a line of clothing called the House of Dereon, all before she even reached her 25th birthday. With Dreamgirls she once again proved she can *work it!* Other famous Black women to *work it* in several careers, include Jada Pinkett Smith, actress, singer (*Wicked Wisdom*), author (*Girls Hold up this World*), and television producer (*All of Us*). And don't forget Queen Latifah, the rapper, singer, spokesperson, cover girl, fashion designer and movie producer.

Now we know you might be saying: "yeah, but they are famous and have the means to do whatever they what to do." But Sisters, don't be fooled, superstars are not the only ones equipping themselves for what-ever the turbulent economy dishes out. Their non-famous counterparts are doing the same. Some of our savviest professional Sisters have also taken it upon themselves to be "Jill of All Trades and Mistress of her Destiny" either because of, or in spite of, the many recent, unexpected, and drastic changes in the economy and in the job market. And, whether you realize it or not, you too can work successfully in more than one career.

To be clear, when referring to careers in this chapter we are intentionally focusing on professions as opposed to jobs. A good frame of reference would be to consider a career as something that could stand on its own, with respect to your resume, your experience, a substantial portion of your time, and long term commitment.

If the truth be told, some Black women end up with more than one career out of necessity. For example, some Sisters take on additional jobs in order to cope with an impending or recent layoff, to manage an unexpected financial problem, or simply to make ends meet. Often times their main objective is to maintain financial obligations, even if it means the quickest way to putting food on table is a low skilled, low paying, ungratifying job. Any of these situations or other unexpected challenges could happen to any of us. Therefore, a Sister who works smarter, not harder, is one who starts preparing right now for that possibility.

If you can help it, having parallel careers should be quite intentional, because there's always another way to use your talents, skills and abilities to pursue a second or third vocation.

Tamla Tymus Scott is a great example of a Sister who enjoys the freedom of pursuing multiple career areas rather than being defined by only one. She is licensed to practice law in North Carolina and Washington, DC, (and has a business doing so), serves as counsel on the House Committee for Homeland Security, is a motivational speaker and a Warm Spirit consultant. How does the 36-year-old wife and mother do it?

"It's not easy but I do it because for me it is fun. I can get bored very easily and I also enjoy variety. Time management and dedication are key. Each of my careers is important to me in terms of self-fulfillment and in terms of my desire to retire to a beach house. I made up my mind that I

would do at least one thing every day to advance my motivational speaking business, my writing business, and my Warm Spirit business."

What is important to Tamla's self-defined success is not how big or small the goals and accomplishments appear to others, but that she satisfies her own purpose for engaging in whatever ventures she decides. As it should be!

Have you ever given any thought to "branching out?" Well now is the time to go for it. The next time someone offers you a compliment like, "Have you ever thought about doing _____ for a living? That just might be the first area you investigate. Remember, don't be overwhelmed by the prospect of going out looking for a side hustle, just open your eyes to what's in front of you and take it one opportunity at a time, being careful not to get in too deep.

Devoted or devoured?

Having multiple careers can be rewarding. It can provide extra loot, a taste of entrepreneurship, give you an outlet for your infrequently used or unused talents, or just provide a bit of variety and challenge to your life.

Take for instance, Dana Legette-Traylor, a dean of fashion marketing and college instructor, who has retail experience that spans over 10 years, *"I have had the pleasure of being invited to participate in various seminars and productions based on my expertise in my profession. I believe this to be the greatest compliment and opportunity to grow professionally. For example, I was contacted by the publicist of a local leading hair salon who had heard of my background and current position. He offered me the opportunity to conduct a seminar that would teach and motivate his 150 employees to increase the sales of private label products. Of course, this was right up my alley. The challenge for me meant that within a three week timeframe, I needed to identify the audience, determine the method of delivery, and fit this into my already hectic schedule. Nevertheless, the session was a success!"*

But Dana will warn anyone that taking on too many extra projects can quickly and almost unnoticeably take on a life of its own. The next thing you know, you might have an additional career or so many competing demands that you feel like you have additional career. Taking on additional careers has to be a well thought out choice and not a forced dive.

Dana has also begun a Doctorate of Business Administration, and she wants to eventually start a consulting firm to assist independent and national retail companies in positioning, branding, customer service training, and the like.

She is aware, however, that as exciting as it can be, having more than one career can also wreak havoc in your life. Sometimes, new ventures require more time or energy than you have to give. Even worse, if you are faced with the competing demands of more than one job, and don't want to give up any of them because you love them almost equally, what then? If you still want to *work it* in more than one career, you will definitely need to step back and examine the situation. Then, ask yourself, "Am I on the road to being devoured?

The authors and the women featured in this chapter believe there is a fine line between a Sister being devoted to her work and being devoured by it. That fine line is mostly impacted by your perspective of how you manage what you do.

Remember Djuanna, the social services program administrator (in the last chapter) who aspires to become an agency director? She realized that Superwoman is a myth and the stressors associated with "doing it all" are self-induced. Let us remind you to avoid getting caught up in The Superwoman Syndrome and stop thinking that the more you do, the more successful you will be. Instead, as Tamla puts it, "You should just have the desire to cultivate and nurture you gifts in a way that is both time-conscious and energy-conscious."

What's the difference and how can you tell where you lie between being devoted and devoured?

Sisters who are devoted...

- work to live
- keep each job and its responsibilities separate from the other
- don't brag about their accomplishments, they just enjoy what they do
- have time for themselves, their jobs, and their families
- spend extra hours getting their presentation or project just right
- see their "to-do" list as a welcome challenge
- can see the light at the end of the work tunnel
- work to achieve their best
- say "no" for the sake of balance and optimum work performance
- work hard and smart to leave time for play
- maintain a schedule
- understand that they must take time to renew themselves

Sisters who are devoured...

- live to work
- use the "other job" as an excuse for poor performance or attendance
- brag about what they do to convince themselves of their happiness
- never feel like they can get it all done
- try to just finish their work—not perfect it
- see their "to do" list as a dreaded task
- are searching around in the darkness of each professional dilemma
- hope for the best
- say no because they are already juggling too many tasks unsuccessfully
- work hard to have time for play
- struggle with making and keeping a schedule
- don't have time to renew themselves

Don't be discouraged if you find yourself leaning more to being devoured than to being devoted. These fresh perspectives can shed some light on the potential to get where you want to be.

Is it really possible to maintain more than one career and your sanity?

Donna Maria Coles Johnson believes so. *"Nothing is impossible! Consider the 24 hours you have in a day and then plan around them. The devil is in the details of course and the journey will be different for everyone. But, what we all want most is for what matters most to us to come together to form an integrated whole, rather than a balanced whole, where we can pick and choose what we want out of life at any given time, schedule it in, and with all the passion we can muster, enjoy every chaotic minute of it. And then, get up and do it all over again tomorrow!"*

How does one successfully manage competing demands?

Tamla Tymus Scott doesn't try to juggle at all. *"To me, balancing depicts trying to juggle them separately without falling over. I choose to blend my roles whenever possible. I have always loved to write motivational material, but my writing has evolved since I began working on the Hill. Now, I write more op-ed pieces and more political-based material, and that has opened new doors for me."*

How does one avoid crossing that line between being devoted and being devoured?

Dana Legette-Traylor won't commit on-the-spot. *"I might immediately be excited and want to say "YES!", but I never commit until I have had a chance to go back and review my calendar to see if I can make a full commitment to the project. But that doesn't always work, so I consult the people who are close to me. They will be honest and tell me 'Dana, you know you can't do that' or 'Yes, you can and here's how.' Once I have decided to take it on, I create responsibility sheets to fully assess the project and make a task list that will help me accomplish the goal. That also helps me not become overwhelmed by the big picture of the project."*

To sum it up, being devoted instead of devoured means effectively managing your time, tasks, and temperament, while you engage in your chosen trades.

Rules of Engagement

We know that as numerous as the Sisters who strive to have it all, there are those who will go overboard by trying to *do* it all. Therefore here are some tips to safeguard against the common pitfalls of being a "Jill of All Trades and Mistress of *NONE*" by taking on too many separate interests.

- *Love what you do.* It's hard enough to have one job you don't like, don't double your trouble or triple it. You must allow yourself to be fueled by your passion. When things get overwhelming, step back and examine the situation. Do you need an adjustment in your time management, tasks management, or temperament management to increase your feeling of passion to a more acceptable level?

- *Keep up to par in the career that is your bread and butter.* Or, you may find yourself wondering about your next meal. It's easy to get caught up in your passions when they are providing the zest you need in your life. But don't neglect getting done the requisite tasks for being on top of your game when it comes to your primary career.

- *Prioritize your gigs.* When conflicts arise, there should be no decision to be made as to what comes first. Planning your time appropriately and proportionately should prevent most potential problems in this area.

- *Make sure at least one of your gigs is completely flexible.* Keep yourself in a position to accept or refuse an assignment based on your current workload and life goings on, without risking future opportunities. Flexibility can also mean being able to determine when and where the work can be performed. Is it something you can do once the family is asleep or before they awake, whenever you have a day off, or during any hour you find yourself with free time? And, can you do it at the library, in a coffee shop, in your home office or must it be done in a certain place and only at certain times? Don't put yourself in the position of having to maintain more than one rigid schedule. This is most feasible through contract work, freelance work or project work.

❖ *Know when to fold.* When the lows outweigh the highs, let it go! Use the devoted or devoured checklist as a frequent (weekly or monthly) evaluation of where you are and where you need to be. Make copies of it and circle each item as it relates to your current situation. Some weeks or months will be worse than others, but when you see a pattern develop of being more devoured than devoted, address it immediately. Decide what you can do to reverse the trend and DO IT!

❖ *Know what you are getting into.* Figure out before you start what you'll give up by taking on multiple careers and decide if it's worth it. If not, then stay put, and achieve success without making a move.

WORK IT, GIRL! TO-DO LIST

✔ **Create a separate identity for each area of expertise.** Give yourself a job title and identify your area of expertise. Write a separate mission statement, goals and plan for each. Neither your resume nor business cards should be a 'catch-all' marketing tool. If you have a web presence, separate identities may be necessary there too.

✔ **Organize your vision.** Set some structure for spending an appropriate amount of time developing and working in each career area. Your goals should be quantifiable, but not necessarily in the same units. For example, you might determine how many articles per year, how many clients per month, and how many hours per week will spell success for you.

✔ **Establish professional collaborations and personal networks.** Share the load. If you write and know someone with skills in PR, perhaps you can help each other out on different projects or collaborate on a joint project. Personal networks might include friends with whom you can exchange favors, such as purchasing supplies, caring for children, or picking up dry cleaning.

Jill of All Trades— Mistress of Her Destiny!

So you think you are down for the multi-tasking that comes with pursuing multiple career fields. This action plan is designed to empower you to get started or keep it going in a realistic and sensible way.

Who are you? Identify the different areas that you want to or are already pursuing:
(Example: public speaking, painting and pharmacology)

Mentoring   Networking

Selling   Entreprenuer

Which, if any, of these interests has to be your primary focus and why?

Entreprenuer because I don't want to be an employee the rest of my life and I want to create something that will continue a cashflow even when I'm not working.

Record how many hours you need to devote each week to each area of interest:

Entreprenuer 10   Networking 10+

Selling 25+   Selling Mentor 5+

Why do you want to pursue all of these areas?

Because they all create a skill set that will allow me to be successful at what I want to pursue which is early retirement.

Come up with a one sentence description for what you offer and how you can get paid for it. (Example: I am a poet who can earn money by competing in poetry contests.)

I am a motivator and can earn money by writing motivating book a speaking at seminars.

Honestly answer this question for yourself, "How can I do this without being devoured?" .

Proper prior planning and not accepting every engagement to speak when I don't have room on my calendar, but still w/the engagements planned already.

Pursuing several career paths can be challenging. Complete this message to yourself that will empower you in your efforts:

"I can do this, I am _Strengthened by Christ_!"

WORK IT, GIRL! PROFILE OF
CRYSTAL McCRARY ANTHONY

Crystal McCrary Anthony has taken the lyrics "I'm Every Woman" and incorporated them into this dance we call life. Starting out as an attorney, then turning to more artistic pursuits, she is proving that women can excel professionally in more than one area. She's been called attorney, author (*Homecourt Advantage* and *Gotham Diaries*), movie producer (*Dirty Laundry*), and television producer and talk show host (*BET-J*), but in this revealing interview with the authors of *Work It, Girl!* this talented "Jill of All Trades" makes it clear that being a "mom" is just as important.

Six Questions for Crystal McCrary Anthony

1) **WIG:** When you got started in your career did you ever imagine that you would be a lawyer, writer, television and movie producer, and television talk show host?

Crystal M. Anthony: *When I first graduated from law school, I had a coveted position in the entertainment department of a prestigious New York City law firm. For most attorneys, my position would have been a dream job. In many ways it was. My resume had a solid foundation and I had an opportunity to build my contract drafting and negotiating skills working with some of the most accomplished artists of our time. Yet, somehow the work was dissatisfying and became frustrating. The problem for me was that I was representing artists who were making their living creatively, which was what I really wanted to be doing instead of lawyering. Around that time I began reading a book called "The Artist's Way" by Julia Cameron and discovered that I was a "shadow artist" meaning I was shadowing artists in my profession instead of fulfilling my own desire to be an artist myself. Not long after reading this book I took* *a chance and left my law firm determined to write a novel. My first book, "Homecourt Advantage" followed, then "Gotham Diaries" and several magazine pieces in between. Next came the first feature film I produced, "Dirty Laundry," television appearances, then "BET-J" hosting ensued. Before I realized what was happening, I was involved in all of these amazing creative projects. And the funny thing is, none of my creative endeavors, beyond writing, were calculated or even expected for that matter. I would say what I have done in the entertainment industry has come about organically. What has been consistent for me since leaving my law firm and embarking on a creative path has been my openness and commitment to explore a variety of paths in the entertainment industry, even those I never anticipated.*

2) **WIG:** What do you enjoy most about your multi-faceted career?

Crystal M. Anthony: *I most enjoy the ability to create in so many different mediums—to create a fictional world of characters whose stories bring joy or life lessons to readers or to produce a film from beginning to end and nurture it to life, to being a part of a television show like "My 2 Cents," which is an important program for the African-American diaspora, bringing to light issues that are of interest to our community. I also appreciate the flexibility of having a job where I can see my children off to school and arrange my schedule to be home when they return from school.*

3) **WIG:** This chapter is titled "Jill of All Trades – Mistress of Her Destiny!" What does that phrase mean to you?"

Crystal M. Anthony: *The phrase "Jill of All Trades—Mistress of Her Destiny!" means that I have many interests and disciplines that I have worked very hard at and continue to work hard to hone, that I have taken risks and chances propelled by passion, conviction and instinct, believing in myself even when others told me I didn't know what the hell I was doing and had no chance of succeeding.*

69

It means following my heart despite the mistakes and fears peppering my journey. It means living in integrity and authenticity with myself.

4) **WIG:** How do you balance it all, including motherhood?

Crystal M. Anthony: *Truthfully, I don't know if I'm balancing it all particularly with the demands on my time. I try to divide my days between my children and their activities, work—charitable and professional, personal activities, spiritual enrichment. Still, as much as I may accomplish and attempt to be sensitive to all of my responsibilities, I am often left with the question of whether I am spending enough time with my kids. Then I wonder if I have set aside enough time for writing or administrative work or exercising. The balancing act is a delicate, arduous dance.*

5) **WIG:** What advice do you have for women who want to pursue multiple career fields successfully?

Crystal M. Anthony: *My children are six and four years old—the age and mindset where they expect me to spend all of my time with them. As far as they are concerned, I'm never with them enough. The challenge of adequately dealing with their needs is increased because I am divorced and my children's father lives in another state and I have no family support in New York. So, balancing it all is a major undertaking for me. Frankly, I am not always sure whether or not I am successful at it. What I do try is to be mindful of how I am allocating my time and that whatever I do, my children's needs come first. This mindset of "children first" keeps my other projects in perspective. Pursuing multiple career fields? You need to work tirelessly, try on several hats for size, cultivate relationships in all of the industries you have interest, follow-through, keep yourself current and visible, be flexible and proactive.*

6) **WIG:** What, in your opinion, is the difference between "working" and "working it?"

Crystal M. Anthony: *"Working" and "working it?" Hmmm. I don't know if the two concepts need to be different. When I am working hard getting my hustle on, like when I am fielding calls, going to shoots and pitch meetings prepared and looking the part then rushing off to go to my daughter's ballet class or my son's baseball game, then rushing home to change for a black tie dinner where a major sponsor will be in attendance whom I would like to underwrite a show—by my account, that would be considered "working" and "working it."*

For more information on Crystal McCrary Anthony and her upcoming projects visit www.crystalmccraryanthony.com.

CHAPTER 5
Staying Put—
Achieving Success Without
Making a Move

"I always had only one prayer: 'Lord, just crack the door a little bit, and I'll kick it open all the way'."
— Shirley Caesar (award-winning gospel singer)

Is it still possible these days to achieve success while staying with the same employer for years and years? Absolutely! But remember, staying put doesn't mean standing still.

In 2005 Cassandra M. Chandler was appointed Special Agent in Charge of the Federal Bureau of Investigation's Norfolk, Virginia field office. Prior to that, she was the Assistant Director of the Office on Public Affairs. Chandler began her investigative career as an FBI special agent in 1985 and welcomed the excitement of experiencing many different jobs in law enforcement. Among other things, she investigated white-collar crimes, violent crimes, civil rights violations, and supervised teams of other special agents. These experiences soon became the foundation on which she built her career and assisted her as she ascended through the ranks. She became a special agent in charge, a section chief and eventually the first African-American woman to preside over the Training Division in the FBI's 30-year existence as well as the highest-ranking African-American there.

The good news is that Cassandra Chandler doesn't have to be the exception to the rule. The bad news is that not enough Sisters are adequately equipped to take full advantage of organizational longevity. This chapter will describe four major steps of positioning yourself for advancement when you opt to stay put. They are: getting prepared, getting noticed, getting promoted and getting paid.

Getting Prepared

Just because you have been with the same employer for a long time doesn't mean the company owes you anything. In most cases, the bottom line is the dollar. So, moving up will mean showing your value in terms of streamlining operations or improving productivity. But before you can demonstrate how you are a perfect fit for the job you want, you will have to arm yourself with as much information as possible.

To figure out how best to sell yourself, you need to truly understand what your potential employer is buying. Start by surfing the web to find job announcements for the types of jobs you would like to go after. Don't just limit yourself to your employer's web site, peruse web sites of similar employers and large job banks. Print out 5-10 of these announcements and use them as a "cheat sheet" of what skills and key words should be in your resume. If you already meet or exceed the requirements, apply away! Although you used a big picture view of identifying what employers want, remember that one size does not fit all when it comes to writing your resume. Be sure to tailor each resume to fit each position for which you apply. That way you'll only have to make minor tweaks before it is ready to go.

There is a real possibility that your job interest lies in positions for which you are not quite qualified and you'll need to take up the slack of your shortcomings. If that turns out to be the case, then visit your HR department to find out what company-sponsored training is available. You could also check to see if your employee benefits include payment of professional development outside the company. You may be pleasantly surprised to learn about tuition reimbursement, payment of memberships to professional associations, or sponsorship of classes or workshops in your community or online.

If your employer pays for your professional development, give him or her a return on the investment, not just a receipt for an expense. Bring back handouts or summarize notes from the training. Or, if you offer to

74

do a presentation to demonstrate how you (and your co-workers) can put the new material to use, you would give your employer even more for his or her money. As an added bonus, you'll have the opportunity to show off your presentation skills in preparation for your new job. If your employer does not pay for your training, take the initiative to invest in yourself to show commitment to your own career development. In either case, document the fact that you completed the training and keep track of any contributions you make to the workplace as a result of having completed it. These are the types of things that will later make you stand out amongst fellow applicants.

In addition to identifying your shortcomings as they relate to job skills, it is just as important to solicit feedback about your work, your work style, and other potential areas for improvement. It may be difficult to swallow constructive criticism, so ask for it in small doses and don't become defensive or emotional.

Getting Noticed

The main purpose of this section is to help you create the reality of you being in the position you want. This means it is imperative that the people above you are able to imagine you as their colleague rather than their subordinate, and that your peers are able to envision you in a position of higher authority. Companies are becoming less willing to take risks. Many are not just looking for the perfect candidate, but are looking for the perfect *in-house* candidate. This could be your big chance to take your professional development into your own hands.

Patricia Washington has been with a well known medical insurance company in Massachusetts for 30 years. She never planned to be with the same employer for so long, but her success with the company moved her into positions of greater responsibility. With greater responsibility came greater compensation so she was not compelled to seek employment elsewhere. Of the 14 positions she has held there, she only formally applied for two of them. OK, so her employer had something to offer Pat, right? Well Pat also had something to offer her employer. She took the responsibility for an active role in her own professional development. "*I stayed abreast of industry changes, company strategic initiatives and new ventures. I networked internally and externally as well as attended workshops, conferences, courses, and the like to learn about everything from leadership development to mentoring."* Pat also volunteered to participate on committees and workgroups, both internally and externally. These activities were a great way for her to meet new people, build a network of a variety of people, improve her communication skills and hone her strategic planning skills.

What's important here is the quality, not the quantity of the professional development efforts. Like Pat, be selective and don't stretch yourself too thin. Choose activities and projects that will increase your visibility, help you grow as a professional and provide the opportunities for you to document solid contributions to your team.

Mentoring relationships should be considered an opportunity for professional development, too, so have a mentor *and* be a mentor.

"The mentor who had the most significant impact on my professional career helped me understand how to navigate within the company and helped me to understand the value of networking within the company as well as outside of the company. She was also the first person to give me candid feedback on things that I didn't do so well but would need to improve upon if I wanted to advance my professional career. She introduced me to key leaders within the company and encouraged me to join community service organizations as well as seek positions on community service boards. The benefits to me were invaluable. Without this mentor's insight and support, I would not have pursued some of the positions that I have had over the years. It was through her mentoring that I was able to build my confidence, present myself in a more professional manner and reach out for help when I needed it. The key to our lasting relationship is our respect for each other and our ability to maintain confidential information." Pat has also eagerly "given back" by mentoring a number of young and seasoned professionals. In supporting other professionals in this way, she points out that she benefits by gaining more insight into how to lead the new generation of professionals.

Along with attaining that insight to successfully lead others, you should also strive to attain more skill sets than what you already have. We suggest that you make a point to volunteer for special projects, initiate solutions to current problems, and demonstrate your potential leadership skills by doing things that are different from what you are already good at doing. Stretching yourself into new realms of experience will be the very thing that prepares you for unexpected challenges and opportunities. Remember again to document your work, accomplishments, and overall contributions so it will be on-hand when you are ready to apply for new jobs. Don't seek the limelight for everything you do, but make sure you get credit for your work.

Make Contacts Count

We are not going to let you forget the small thing that makes a BIG impact—making internal contacts count. This is especially true for co-workers who are in different departments and at different worksites. Those colleagues will be less likely to have difficulty imagining the "new you" than those with whom you work every day. If you effectively networked during the early stages of your research then you already have a few contacts that might be helpful to you now. They may let you know when positions become available in their departments. There is also the possibility of their referring you to other hiring managers. Or, if they currently hold a job similar to the one for which you want to apply, they might be able to give you feedback on your resume, or discuss a real "day in the life" of someone who does the job you want to have. This will be the time to establish relationships and nurture them. Keep in touch with a few selected persons without being a pest. You never want people to go running in the opposite direction when they see you coming.

We suggest that you expand your network by seeking additional contacts outside of your organization. Look for professional organizations and associations as well as local groups of business persons in your field. Not sure where to find them? Start with the Chamber of Commerce. If possible, attend some of the meetings of these groups and consider becoming a member of one or two of them. Be aware that each of these groups will have its own personality, level of expectations with respect to *active* participation, membership fees, etc. So don't join too soon. Take your time to find the right group for you. During this phase would be a great time to move from informal networking to arranging networking interviews. It will be important that a few key people understand your goal. Make a note of which of them seem genuinely interested enough to help you achieve it. Remember the saying: "Who you know and what you know are important, but the biggest payoff comes with who knows you!"

Getting Promoted

There are many ways to move around within the company. You can expand your current job, create a new job, find your own opportunities or identify company-wide internal openings and apply for them. In either case, there are three main things to accomplish: show you are the candidate of choice, brush up on your business etiquette skills, and take charge of the interview.

Show You Are the Candidate of Choice

Although you are an internal candidate and may very well be the best person for the job, don't presume that your current resume will demonstrate that you are the candidate of choice. Put into it as much work as possible so that it is able to withstand even the greatest scrutiny. In fact, you may need to write a new resume rather than just updating your old one. How can you tell what is the best strategy? If you are seeking a position that would very obviously be the next step up, then a chronological resume might work best. By listing all your previous positions and your accomplishments in each of them, your resume tells the story of your progression. It leads the reader to see you in the new position as the next logical step.

Conversely, the chronological resume is not an effective tool if the job for which you are applying is completely unrelated to your past positions. In fact, it may give the impression that you are completely UNQUALIFIED for the position. Career changers will most likely benefit from using functional resumes to strut their stuff. This resume format allows you to break down your accomplishments into three or four major transferable skills that would be important for the new job. This targeted approach allows you to hone in on exactly what the job calls for, as discovered in your research. It will be necessary to pull out those vacancy announcements you found in the research phase and read them to identify the key qualifications. Vacancy announcements might read: "Must have project management, training, and supervisory skills." If so, then at a minimum, you must address those as your functional skills if you are to prove you are the right person for the job.

Functional resumes may seem more difficult to write mostly because you may not be familiar with them. However, you are likely to have noticed a pattern during your job search that most of the jobs in which you are interested require similar skill sets. Therefore, once you identify the 3-5 skills most in demand for those positions, you can pre-write the functional skill paragraphs into a master document and with the simple "cut and paste" process you can use the appropriate ones for each application, and in the applicable sequence. Then, all you will have to do is make whatever edits are necessary to finish off a resume tailored just for that particular job. An added benefit to using a functional resume is that you can use accomplishments from all areas of your past experiences including volunteer work, hobbies, part-time employment, etc. The goal of this format is to emphasize the fact that you have a substantial number of accomplishments in certain skill sets. You don't have to indicate from where and when you accumulated your accomplishments (as in a chronological resume).

Business Etiquette Tips

The further upward you intend to climb on the corporate ladder, the more mealtime schmoozing you'll be likely to do. Whether it be a lunchtime job interview, a dinner meeting with a potential client, networking with a colleague or attending your company's dinner party, the table manners mama taught you may not be enough to keep a competitive edge, so here are a dozen things to keep in mind:

1. No matter how informal the mealtime business meeting might seem, you must maintain the highest level of professional decorum because it *is* still work.
2. You *are* being evaluated on many different aspects: your conversation, your manners, your interaction with others, everything.
3. Take the lead from the host as to when it is time to start and stop talking shop.
4. If things go wrong, a drink is spilled, the food is not good, a fork is dropped, remain calm. Work with the wait staff to resolve any and all problems, don't sweat the small stuff, and move on!
5. When you are on the clock, alcohol is considered a no-no.
6. Familiarize yourself with place settings so you know which ones to use and when to use them. If you forget, take the lead from your interviewer or host.
7. If you have special dietary restrictions, are a picky eater, or have difficulty making mealtime decisions, get online to view the menu and decide ahead of time what you will order.
8. Order items that are easy to eat and do not have the potential to be messy.
9. Limit the amount of paperwork you bring to the table unless there was a specific request for certain documents.
10. Turn off your cell phone or put it on manner mode (vibrate). If it is absolutely necessary to take or make a call, excuse yourself from the table. NEVER talk on your cell phone at the table.
11. Never use profanity or tell inappropriate jokes.
12. Always send a thank you note to the host.

Take Charge of the Interview

When you are invited to interview for an internal position, it is highly likely your interviewer will know you and your work either personally or from asking others in the company. In either case, don't allow the focus of the interview to be on anything except what might get you hired. It is critical that the interviewer see the "new" you, not the one he or she "knows" with respect to your qualifications for this new job. Below are some tips to avoiding certain traps when interviewing for internal positions.

TRAP: Casual chatting

TIP: Since your employer may automatically feel a connection with you, he or she may be tempted to chat casually. However, keep the initial "how-are-you-doing-these-days" conversation as brief as possible. **Prepare a transition line to move the conversation into the real reason you are there**. *I am doing very well these days and am excited that I have the opportunity to interview for this position. I have done some research on it and have already given thought as to how I would approach it.*

TRAP: Irrelevant work experiences

TIP: Don't get trapped into talking about irrelevant work experiences. When asked about your past accomplishments, it is OK to talk about those from past jobs, but **make sure you connect past achievements to how they will impact your performance in the new job**. *I have volunteered to head several projects and have been recognized for my leadership skills during them. My current manager agrees that my performance on these projects have prepared me well for this supervisory position.*

TRAP: Experience speaks for itself

TIP: Even a star employee must go into the interview prepared to point out what makes her the best person for the job. If you think your experience speaks for itself, you are only half right. Your work ethic speaks for itself. It is up to you to **point out, emphasize, and re-emphasize your**

ability to do this job. *I am glad that you have heard so much about my good attendance and ability to work with anyone. But, allow me to give you specific examples of my training skills since I am applying for the position of professional development trainer.*

TRAP: Two-for-one
TIP: Being heavily dependent upon in your current position may be an issue. Especially if the interviewer is concerned about who will fill your old position. These feelings can taint feelings about you in the new position. This is not a fair concern for him or her to act upon, but you must be prepared to pick up on that and alleviate the concern without becoming a two-for-one. In other words, don't allow yourself to end up working at both positions and only being paid for one of them. Mention your willingness to help select your replacement and train him or her to smooth the transition, but specify a time frame in which this will occur. Whatever you do, don't sell yourself as a two-for-one or you'll end up right back where you started—overworked and underpaid!

TRAP: Underestimate the need to rehearse
TIP: It's easy to presume that you will do fine in the interview since you are a current employee, know many of the hiring managers (or even one of them) and have a great resume. Without realizing it, though, you might be basking in a false sense of confidence that leads to a much lower level of performance in the interview than you intended. Regardless of the situation, you must prepare your responses and practice your interviewing skills. Rehearse answers to questions that you know will be asked such as:

- Tell me about yourself.
- Describe some of your weaknesses and how you are trying to improve them.
- What makes you the best person for the job?

Also, prepare specific examples of your accomplishments that you will want to cite during the interview. Don't make them too fact laden or try to memorize them. Just be familiar enough with the details to have a discussion about them and how they relate to your being the ideal person for the job.

Getting Paid

Position yourself for future promotions. Sometimes lateral moves or downward steps might be necessary to expand your future career opportunities. But realize that this might also mean a change in your salary and benefits, so be prepared to get the very best package you can get. Success with the art of negotiating a higher salary lies in being fully aware of the parameters within which you have to work. Take time to find out the salary range of your intended position(s) and what determines where one falls within that range.

Then make absolutely certain that your resume clearly demonstrates that you exceed the requirements of the job. Point out not only what you have done in the past that you could do in the next job, but also share your plans for what you will do when you get the job. In order to *work it* you MUST think about it. Write about it. Talk about it. Own it! Enthusiasm is contagious. Gain your employer's support by mentioning a few ideas that he or she will want to discuss right now——or as soon as you get that new position and that new level of pay.

If you do not succeed in getting a higher salary, be prepared to negotiate for non-financial rewards based upon your proven record within the company—more time off, company sponsored leadership development training, or an alternative work schedule.

Position Yourself for Longevity. Any Sister who is with the same employer for an extended period of time may find it necessary to make changes in the way she works to accommodate changes in her life. If you are among the many Sisters who have prayed for a way to better balance familial and professional commitments, then it may be necessary for you to find a new way to work, without jeopardizing your professional image.

For 15 of her nearly 21 years working at a college in Boston, Janet Costa Bates, Associate Director of the Career Center, has held a job share position and wouldn't trade it for the world. *"Job sharing allows me*

83

to maintain a balance between my family and my work. It also allows me to pursue other opportunities, which include writing and teaching. On the other hand, admits the wife and mother of two, working three days a week is frustrating since I often have 'full-time' expectations of myself." That high level of self-expectation is probably a key factor in her success with this alternative work arrangement.

Janet sought a job share position after her children were born. Getting approval of her proposal took preparation, research and extensive negotiation. And her persistence paid off because she got the job share opportunity and later, a promotion. Janet was fortunate that as a result of her promotion she only had to change job share partners. She wasn't also faced with having to choose between having a job share position and advancing in her career.

Job sharing is one of several alternative work arrangements Sisters might want to explore as a work-life option. **Alternative work arrangements** refer to almost any deviation from the standard 9 to 5 workday in an employer's work location performing the normal responsibilities of one's position. These arrangements typically are beneficial to both the employer and employee, and can be permanent or temporary.

As in Janet's case, job sharing is when two part-time employees share one full-time job, usually working on opposite days and meeting weekly to ensure continuity, if the two jobs are the same (two accountants). Job sharing can also occur when two part-time people share one full-time slot, but two different jobs, a situation that is usually initiated as a budgetary advantage to the employer. Two other popular alternative work arrangements include **flextime** and compressed **work week**. Using **flextime** means you work hours that are different from the normal eight-hour day, 40-hour work week to accommodate your life outside work; it usually only involves a slight modification to your basic start time or end time. Having a compressed **work week** means working more hours on fewer days. It usually allows for at least one more day off than the normal weekend. Examples include: four ten-hour days and one day off during a week; eight nine-hour days, one eight-hour day, and one day off over two weeks; and three thirteen hour workdays with four days off in one week.

If you think you can better work it by working out an alternative work arrangement, don't just assume your employer will agree. You'll have to make a good case for it. Read on to the next chapter to learn how to propose a win-win situation for you and your employer. You, too, might become a Sister who makes working from home work for you!

WORK IT, GIRL! TO-DO LIST

✔ **Get it in writing**. Now that you have decided to remain with your current employer and move up within that organization it is time to secure the job description of your desired position. Here's the deal. Identify where you want to go in your organization and be more specific than just wanting to be in management. For example, you might determine that you want to be the Vice President for Internal Affairs. It doesn't matter if someone already has that job or that you are not qualified for it yet. If that is where you want to be, get it in writing. Most human resources departments have copies of job descriptions on file and have no problem with sharing them. If you don't want to give a reason for why you want it, just say that you or someone you know is doing research in the field. Or to have complete anonymity, secure a description of the same job from another organization if they also require the same knowledge, skills and abilities for the job. Seeing what you want to do in writing can be your guide for what you need to do to make it happen!

✔ **Solicit feedback.** Most organizations conduct annual reviews or employee evaluations. Take your most recent one and make a list of areas in need of improvement and areas in which you must maintain stellar performance. If you have had no formal written review of your job performance, request one in a manner that your employer can respect. You could ask, for example, "What do you feel are my strengths and weaknesses in my current position? I'd like to determine how close I am to excelling in my current responsibilities." We don't know many employers who wouldn't be impressed with an employee who wants to excel at work. Finally, be prepared for feedback that may not be what you are looking for and don't make excuses. The bottom line: no matter how great you may think you are, your boss' opinion really does matter.

✔ **Be a buddy.** Being socially savvy at work could be as simple as letting your co-workers know that you are a "team player" by your actions and not just by what you say. Offering to cover a meeting for one of your counterparts or holding open the door when someone is weighed down with work materials can go a long way. So can a smile. It's great to be liked at work and it's also great to reap the benefits of that status.

✔ **Don't bite the hand that hires you.** The human resources department is definitely a good place to network. Having a good relationship with HR personnel can be beneficial for many reasons, including being in the know when an opening that you are interested in is about to be posted. Some people make the mistake of blaming the staff in the HR Department about unsatisfactory things in their work record. Remember, most of those reports originate somewhere else, HR usually only maintains the record. They can also give you answers to any employee concerns you may have in the workplace.

✔ **Don't get rusty.** There are inexpensive ways to be *interview ready* and *employment trend knowledgeable*. You could take continuing education courses to freshen up your resume or fine-tune your interviewing skills. Or, be a 'student' of current business trends and current events. You can accomplish the same by reading in each of those areas. Instructional books can cost you as little as $14.95 (or less) and a few hours of your time; however, the rewards will be priceless.

ACTION PLANNER
Staying Put—
Achieving Success Without
Making a Move

You have decided to stay put and achieve success where you are. Now it's time to map out the plan for your ascension to the top!

Regardless of your current job title, salary and job description you can dream big. What position at your company do you really want to have?

V.P. of Sales

Provide a one sentence description of your "dream job."

Mentoring + inspiring Sales team to exceed goals in generating revenue for the company.

What knowledge, skills and abilities are required to put you on track for this promotion? Be specific by including degrees, training and/or experience that is required.

Mainly more experience in Sales management is what I need since I already have the degrees + some experience. Also continued education in this field.

Who are the person(s) at your company that you need to network with, show you skills, and ask for help to get what you want at work?

Ron Robear
Juanita Keller
Carol Wilson

Research your company's mission statement and make it the basis for writing your resume and acing the interview. What is the mission of your organization?

(If there is no formal mission statement, research the history and organizational goals of the company to help you create one. Have the courage to share it with management.)

MISSION STATEMENT:

_____

_____

_____

There is always room for self-improvement. Think about it and list ways that you can enhance your professional image.

More assertive _____   _____

Don't over analyze _____   _____

Procrastination _____   _____

It's a common interview question and a very necessary one to assess where you want to go, "WHERE DO YOU WANT TO BE IN FIVE YEARS?" Use the space to journal your answer and use it as you continue to craft your plan to achieve success without making a move.

WORK IT, GIRL! PROFILE OF
MONICA KAUFMAN PEARSON

Monica Kaufman Pearson is, without a doubt, one of Atlanta's most recognizable faces. Some would call her an "institution" in Atlanta because she has been on the air at WSB-TV for over thirty years. She anchors Channel 2 Action News at 5, 6 and 11 p.m. Monday through Friday. The award-winning news anchor started at the station in 1975. She made history as the first Black and first woman to anchor the evening news in Atlanta. She is nationally known for her success in the field of journalism. The authors of *Work It, Girl!* caught up with her to give our readers some insight on achieving success without making a move.

Six Questions For Monica Kaufman Pearson:

1) **WIG:** Your "staying power" in your position at WSB-TV is something that few news anchors achieve. How have you stood the test of time in one of the top media markets in the country?

Monica Kaufman Pearson: *I never take my career for granted. When I first arrived I spoke to as many schools and civic organizations as I could. I spoke at women's day programs and judged contests. I sang at church programs and sporting events. I appeared just about everywhere I could, representing the station, so viewers got to know me and not just what they saw on television. One year I did almost 250 appearances, many of them on weekends and before I came to work. When people get to know you up close and personal, touch you, share a meal with you, it builds loyalty. You become a member of their family, a friend. But at the same time, I served on the boards of some organizations, including United Way, which got me working in the Black and White communities. I also tutored in a program now called Cities in Schools. And, of course, I did my job* *well; first as a reporter and then as an anchor. I constantly critiqued my work and worked on being me, not an imitation of Barbara Walters or Walter Cronkite. Over the years I have decreased my appearances but I still do them. I volunteer to read at an elementary school once a week and have done so for five years. I serve on fewer boards but do still lend my name to organizations. I do what I've always done but not as much of it. And I still review my tapes to make sure I'm not falling into bad habits on the air. I try to keep it fresh and talk to viewers, rather than read to them. I've lasted because I work at being the best I can be. And I've learned to be comfortable in my own skin, no matter what others say about me.*

2) **WIG:** Do you believe that you would have been as successful in your field if you would have moved around to various markets or cities. Why or why not?

Monica Kaufman Pearson: *Yes, I think I could have been just as successful elsewhere because people like to watch people they know and have a vested interest in. I was not guaranteed success. When I came to WSB in August of 1975, women and Blacks anchored the noon shows, weekends and early mornings, but there were no women anchoring the bread and butter shows, then 6 and 11 p.m. Monday through Friday. It was an all White male affair. I was the first to integrate the evening news, as a woman and a Black. Some Blacks didn't think I was black enough and wanted to see a huge afro. Many Whites thought I was too black and didn't want an "N" on the air. There was far more criticism than praise. But because I joined a church, got involved in the community and had a base of support, I was able to "tough it out." Everyone should build a support system outside the workplace.*

3) **WIG:** What advice can you provide to women who want to achieve career success without making a move or changing organizations?

Monica Kaufman Pearson: *If you want to move up, rather than out of an organization, you've got to make yourself "valuable." First, do your job exceptionally well. Don't be afraid to take on new tasks and learn new skills that make your company better. Work in the community and then share that involvement with your company newspaper. Management likes to see one of their own doing good in the community because it says, we don't just make our money here, we give back.*

Stay out of office gossip. Every dog who brings a bone, wants to take one back. You can't be misquoted if you don't participate. When people ask you what you think about such and such, or if they complain, tell them they ought to ask the people involved and not you. You can do it sweetly. Stay above the mess. And, always look at the job postings. There may be something there that will move you to another level, another experience, another reason to show you are a better employee than someone else.

4) **WIG:** You have very loyal viewers and fans in Atlanta, how has this popularity impacted your life?

Monica Kaufman Pearson: *This is the only area that is not fun when you are a Mom. My daughter played soccer and basketball and was in gymnastic meets. I had a rule: No autographs or conversations about what I do until after Claire was finished and she and I had hugged or talked. I had to be Mommy first. While many people are very nice, there are the haters who want to tear you down. I've learned the difference between constructive and destructive criticism. I know which to ignore. I set boundaries. No work stuff when I'm worshipping at church. Don't call me at home about a news story. I need downtime too. I've learned to tell people that. When people try to talk me into things by pulling the "you're one of the most successful Blacks or women and you need to....." I cut them off. I tell them I need to take care of me. So, I have to limit what I do to preserve my health, my marriage, my relationships with my* *daughter and my mother. Most times people want to talk to me about my hair. I change it all the time and sometimes viewers hate it and want to fuss about it. I just say, 'my hair is an accessory and just like the weather, it will change.' You must have a sense of humor to survive when you are in a very public job.*

5) **WIG:** How do you define success?

Monica Kaufman Pearson: *Career success, to me, is doing what you love, on your own terms. It has nothing to do with money, market size, or recognition. For me it has to do with making a difference in the lives of people, telling stories that make people want to help, and having fun in the process.*

6. **WIG:** What, in your opinion, is the difference between "working" and "working it?"

Monica Kaufman Pearson: *"Working" is just that: showing up for that 8 hour stint, doing just what is asked of you and dreaming about what you're going to do when you retire. "Working it" is putting your personality, your initiative, your imagination, your time, your humor, and your style into your passion….your career choice. It's doing what it takes to make you say, 'That was a day well spent!' Work is just that, a four letter word. "Working it" is massaging who you are into what you do. My 83-year-old Mother, Hattie Edmondson, has said it another way for the 59 years of my life, 'It's what you do, with what you have, that makes you what you are.'*

CHAPTER 6

Make Working from Home Work for You

"Everything changes—your profession, your life. You have to antici-pate it, accept it and create a plan to reinvent your role and yourself."
-Lita Cunningham as HR Executive

When Desiree McCullough, a reimbursement manager for a home health care company, adopted her first child she didn't have enough vacation time to take a three-month maternity leave. The North Carolina-based professional also dreaded returning to mounds of paperwork. Therefore, she posed a win-win solution to her administrator. She proposed a work alternative that would allow her to come into the office twice weekly to run financial reports so that she could prepare the monthly statements at home.

Desiree's innovative thinking didn't just save her company time. It also saved them the hassle and money of training someone to do the job temporarily. The peace of mind of knowing that her maternity leave would not cause any change in the departmental processes she was instrumental in establishing was also a plus.

"It turned out that I could get a lot more work done at home because I wasn't interrupted as much as I am at work. Plus, I could determine my own work schedule even if that meant working late at night or during the baby's naptime. Working from home, even on a part-time basis, is wonderful. I believe that if people were able to work shorter weeks for the same pay they would actually be more productive!"

How many times have you dreamed of waking up, slipping into your fluffiest slippers, and working from home? OK, you might have to take the kids to school, but you could return right back there and get down to business—focused, energized, and ready to take on the world. No commuting, no figuring out what to wear, just jumping right in and getting the job done. In fact, like Desiree, you could probably get more done before noon time than you would if you went to the office. Think about it. If you took an inventory of how you spend your time at work, you might just see that it doesn't compare to what you COULD do if you worked at home.

According to the results of a 2005 survey of the International Telework Association and Council millions of people work outside their employer's office. In fact, the survey showed a 30% increase of telecommuters in the year preceding the survey. It also states that there are 26.1 million people who work from home at least one day per month and at least 22.2 million people who work from home at least once per week.

Sound intriguing? Then this could be the time to consider redesigning how you work.

A New Way to Work?

Working at home on a part-time temporary basis, such as with Desiree's three-month maternity leave, is one of many situations in which working from home makes sense for the employee and for the employer. But what about working from home occasionally as a permanent arrangement? If you are a mother or caregiver of other family members, working from home would help you more easily meet your personal commitments to your loved ones. Or, if you drive a significant distance to the workplace or travel in considerable traffic each day, you could actually "create" more hours in your day by working from home once or twice per week instead of commuting to work. After all, when you look at the numbers, thirty minutes of commuting to work and thirty minutes commuting home, per day, equates to 250 hours per year (with the exclusion of a two-week vacation), if you work five days each week. That's about 31 eight-hour work days! Would those extra hours put you in a new frame of mind?

Of course it would; but, as usual, it's time for a reality check, and we've got your back. Yes, the benefits of working from home are obvious for the employees: fewer commuting hours, fewer distractions, more (potentially) free time, less stress, greater flexibility, greater ability to schedule repair calls, medical appointments, and on and on. But what about the company? Does your employer really benefit? Absolutely! What employer wouldn't benefit from having a happier, more productive employee who thinks the world of the company just because they feel more productive and in control of their life? Not to mention, happy employees tend to be more willing to go the extra mile when the need arises and they have a positive impact on recruitment and retention of other good employees.

Another reality check is that your well-balanced life MAY be a "hard sell" to your boss. It may not automatically translate into something great for the company. So, if you are thinking about redesigning how you work, you'll have to "get it together, or leave it alone".

When the benefits to the employer aren't as obvious as they were in Desiree's case you've got to *work it*! It will be up to you to develop a convincing proposal and to present it either in writing, in person, or better yet, both.

The good news is that, these days, more and more employers are becoming amenable to employees working from home. The bad news? They are not likely to advertise this fact or to have a formal work-at-home program already in place. Instead, employees who work from home are most often those who: have been on the job for a while; have proven themselves to be valuable employees; and are able to convince the employer that it would be a win-win situation to allow them to work from home. How can you do it?

Step 1: Design Your Plan

From this point on you'll need to start thinking of this idea of working from home as a formal arrangement. That being said, it is important to give it a name. Let's refer to it as teleworking (which is also known as telecommuting). By definition teleworking involves the use of telephones, computers, fax machines and other such equipment at a place other than your normal worksite, in order to complete the same job duties you would do if you commuted to work via car, bus, or train. On average, telecommuters do not work from home full-time. Many of them work from home one to three days per week.

Step 2: Evaluate the Whole Situation

Could working at home work for you? Be forewarned, it's not for everyone. There are four main things you should know before you get into a situation that might put your professional credibility or employment status at risk: know your job, know your boss and colleagues, know yourself, and know your resources.

Know your job.

How much of your job could be done from home as easily as it is done at the office? It is unrealistic to think that your entire job could be done working from home in isolation and without interaction with others. The easiest way to present your case for working at home is to break down your job into which tasks are most doable at home. Whether presenting your case for teleworking permanently or on a temporary basis, your best bet is to identify tasks that are measurable, yield tangible products, and require large amounts of your time or concentration. For example, could you write reports, prepare presentations, or update online data? Or, you may opt to include time for vital tasks that don't require face time or your being tied to a particular workspace. These activities include answering e-mail, making phone calls and participating in conference calls.

You will know, based on the fact that you likely have been with this employer for while, which tasks you should consider for duties you can conduct at home. And although it might be easier to think about the tasks you would *prefer* to do, you must truly give thought to what will make the most sense for your employer. After all, this work arrangement can't come across as something that just makes your life easier. Finally, developing this work arrangement should not become a guessing game for your employer. How you plan to work must be clear, concise, and definite when presented to him or her.

"*When I went into the office, it was to accomplish specific tasks*" (not to socialize), said Desiree. "*I would open my mail, meet with my administrator and give her a list of things I had worked on as well as discuss any problems or issues that needed to be addressed. I would also meet with my staff once a week to talk about issues that pertain to them. I ran additional reports that I was unable to run from home because the system I had for dialing and was very slow.*"

Clearly, Desiree planned for accomplishing specific tasks when she went into the office. She ran audits, reviewed the data and checked the posted entries while on site. If she had not, her month-end financials would not have been available for the Board. Her administrator agreed that would not have been an acceptable result.

Know your boss and colleagues.

Working at home can be challenging if the people you work with, and for, are not supportive or simply object to your arrangement. Will your boss and co-workers still take you seriously if you are working from a distance? How much time is enough "face time" to counter the possible impact of being out of sight and out of mind? You'll have to spend some time identifying what might be the main concerns of others in your workplace and address them in a positive manner. The most common concerns tend to be those that involve *accessibility* to you, *predictability* of your schedule, and *continuity* of the goals and objectives of your department, team, or office.

Let's face it, the people in your office want to be comfortable that they can reach you when needed. They need to know the best ways to get in touch with you and how responsive you will be to them, period. Tell them the core work hours you will be available to them. Let them know that that you will return their phone calls and e-mails. Commit to providing any documents they need in a timely manner. They want to know that you still share their goals and objectives in getting the job done. In other words, take the time to state up front that your change in your work location will in no way disturb the groove of others who work with you or for you. The truth is, if you don't already perform to this high level of standard when you are in the office, it's not likely that they will think you'll be able to do it when you're out of the office.

We suggest two final points to aid in your success. First, it will benefit you to find out if there are others in your company who telecommute. They could serve as an excellent resource for you. Second, if your company is dedicated to environmental causes you might consider mentioning the reduction in air pollution and the conservation of fuel.

Know yourself.

In order to do this successfully, it is crucial that you acknowledge which aspects of your personality and work style will make you most productive in a work-at-home situation. Conversely, you must also acknowledge which of them will hinder your productivity. For instance, are you tough enough to avoid distractions even if you are a softy at heart or are normally accessible to the people in your personal life? If not, there is nothing wrong with that. Just be aware that you *will* have to set some boundaries up front, for yourself and for them.

Melissa Washington-Harris, a thirty-something self-employed publicist and event planner, toyed with the idea of working from home when she was six months pregnant with her second child. She wanted more time and energy to spend with her family. However, she worked at a PR firm in a very demanding position with long hours. Another grueling dynamic of the situation was having an unmarried boss who had no children and no consideration for her family obligations. All of this made her question whether she really wanted to continue putting that much of herself into building someone else's company.

Melissa knew up front that in order to make working from home work for her, she would have to focus on two things. 1) She would have to take on projects that fit her work style and preferences. 2) She would have to set some boundaries at home.

"Given the choice I prefer short-term projects, like PR for events or writing press releases and press kits, because I am able to get the job done in a short amount of time. I also know that, in my experience, the longer a

project is the more potential there is for me to lose interest in it depending on the nature of the job," she said.

She recognized her need to limit interaction with her loved ones when she was working. She also knew that it would be important to limit her accessibility to clients when she wasn't. Therefore, Melissa put some rules in place.

"My children know that if the door to my office is closed, I am working and should not be disturbed unless it is an emergency. It was up to me to help friends and family understand that just because I work at home, it does not mean that I am available to chitchat or to be a backup babysitter. I also realized that the danger of your clients knowing you work from home is that they feel they have access to you 24/7. At first I really got annoyed about having to deal with this until I finally got it in my head that I have the power to control it. Now, when the phone rings, I check the caller ID. During my office hours, I pretty much only answer for clients and school or day care. After 6:00 p.m. I only take personal calls."

Melissa's rules allow her to achieve something greater than work balance. Following those types of rules can lead to greater life balance. Working at home shouldn't mean that you are constantly working. A "perpetual office" can take away from your love life and stop you from keeping the home fires burning with your husband, boyfriend or significant other. If you're a mother your children may think that you put work before them. This arrangement is not designed to make you work too hard, it's your opportunity to "work smart!"

Know your resources

Depending upon your job, working at home could be difficult without the proper equipment. So, take the time to put everything in place before you begin this arrangement to ensure that the transition will be as smooth as possible. In some cases employers may be willing to provide you with a computer, telephone, copier, scanner, and other necessary items. In fact, nowadays, many people work from laptops and cell phones. If you fall into this category make the portability of your equipment a big advantage to "selling" a work at home situation.

If you're not fortunate enough to have office equipment provided by your employer, you will need to decide whether this situation will limit the success of your work-at-home arrangement. And, if so, figure out what you are willing to do about it. If you already have the basics of a home office you might consider using your own equipment for the job. And, perhaps your employer will be willing to reimburse you for less costly items such as ink cartridges and paper.

If, like Melissa, you decide to work from home for yourself rather than for someone else consider your clients and contacts to be part of your resource pool. It would be a smart move to make sure they, too, are in place as resources before you begin your new way to work. Commit yourself to utilizing them as such since they are every bit as necessary to your success as having the right equipment.

"If I had to do it again, the one thing I might do differently is to make sure key contacts knew me on a first name basis. I spent more months than I care to remember trying to develop relationships with key people. If I'd spent a little more time doing that, before I took the plunge to work for myself, then things would've been a little easier. In PR, like in many other fields, success is built on relationships. In the beginning I knew I could do the work, but I let my fears get in the way a few times. Now, that is no longer the case. If I want a particular client, I go for it. No questions asked. I network whenever and wherever necessary to make sure I have everything in place to work from home successfully."

Step 3: Go for the Gusto

Take no shortcuts when you are ready to make a formal request to work from home. Go for the gusto and "bring the heat". Make it difficult for your employer to say "no" by proposing a win-win situation. The best approach is to do your homework, have a well-thought out plan of action and communicate it as professionally as you would any other project.

A key point here is that the format of the proposal is not nearly as important as the content. Here is a checklist of what to include:

+ Provide a **clear explanation** of your plan for implementing an arrangement to work at home.

- Focus on the **benefits to your employer** (think: increased productivity, efficiency and effectiveness).
- Don't forget to demonstrate **your value to the company** by pointing out your specific contributions, accomplishments and past performance.
- Point out the **characteristics and work style** for which you are most well-known at work. Make the case for those being the same reasons that make you an employee who can maintain high standards when working from home.
- List the **measurable and tangible work products** you will provide as a means of your accountability.
- Clarify your **accessibility, work schedule and commitment to shared goals**.
- Outline your **equipment needs** or willingness to provide your own to demonstrate the feasibility of maintaining your responsibilities to other members of the team.
- Forecast and prepare to **address objections** from your managers and co-workers.
- Offer to work at home on a **trial basis** and meet periodically to determine the effectiveness of this arrangement as well as discuss necessary adjustments.

To find sample templates of proposals and additional content recommendations, visit www.judywolf.com or www.workathomesuccess.com. Other informative web sites are: www.workoptions.com and www.workingfromanywhere.org.

When all is said and done, if you succeed in creating a new way to work, be prepared for the possibility that there may be some resistance initially. Be willing to remain flexible in order to keep EVERYONE (you, your family, and your employer/colleagues/clients) comfortable with this situation. After all, wasn't that your goal from the start? The work-at-home strategies presented in this chapter WILL work, whether you use them to contribute to your employer's bottom line or your own, even if you decide to turn a hobby into a career!

WORK IT, GIRL! TO-DO LIST

✔ **Document your time at work.** Before you propose the new work arrangement you should keep a log for three months, if possible, to document how you spend your time at work. This will help you best determine what tasks could be done at home. Also, include in it a list of your regularly occurring deadlines, your work products, accomplishments, challenges, etc.

✔ **Plan your work days.** Once you have a clear picture of your workload, use it to plan your workdays at home, just like you would do at the office. Neglecting to do so could set you up for failure. The flexibility of working from home should not turn into working whenever you get around to it. Set your hours and stick to them. This will also help you not feel compelled to work around the clock when at home. Include time for lunch and breaks to keep your mind as fresh as possible.

✔ **Set up a home office that works for you.** It is important to work where you feel the most effective. Designate a space to work and put in it everything you need to be comfortable—but not "too comfortable". Although this area should be your primary workspace, allow yourself a change of scenery. Working in different places throughout your home can help you to re-focus and re-energize when needed. Figure out exactly what it would take to fully equip you to take care of business. Use a separate telephone line from the one your family uses and don't allow others to answer it. Allow yourself the luxury to have voice mail on this line so you can have more control of your time and concentration.

✔ **Buyer beware.** If you have bought into the possibility of working from home, buyer beware. Don't be too casual about it. Wearing lounge wear, working in the bedroom or on the couch, watching television, and trying to do chores while you work may be detrimental to your productivity.

✔ **Honestly assess your effectiveness.** If after a few weeks you are not maintaining an appropriate level of performance, don't be afraid to re-evaluate whether this arrangement will work for you. In the long run, your professional credibility must remain a priority. Remember, your goal in this arrangement is to replace an undesirable work arrangement with one that is better for you personally. It is not to get by doing the bare minimum. Be aware that this arrangement could actually complicate your life at home, too, so don't be afraid to honestly assess that aspect as well.

Make Working from Home Work for You

If you are looking for a way to work from home this document will help you keep track of all the information you need to work your plan.

List the key components of your current job and circle the tasks and duties that can be completed in a home-based work environment.

_____   _____

_____   _____

_____   _____

_____   _____

What schedule would REALLY work for your teleworking opportunity? Create one that would make this an attractive offer to your employers. Be sure to include an adequate amount of face time, for example, to attend the weekly sales meeting. Remember the key considerations: accessibility, predictability and continuity. If you will be your own boss create the proposed schedule with the same considerations in mind for your clients.

Detailed Proposed Schedule:

_____

_____

_____

_____

Make a list of the things you will need for a professional workspace/home office:

_____   _____

_____   _____

_____   _____

Complete the checklist contained in the chapter, highlighting the following key points to include in your proposal: *clear explanation of your plan; the benefits to your employer; your value to the company; characteristics of your work style; measurable and tangible work products; accessibility, work schedule, and commitment to shared goals; equipment needs; address possible objections; and a trial basis offer.*

Complete the *Work It, Girl!* To-Do List.

"Work It, Girl! If you really want to work from home, *believe it* so you can *achieve it*!"

WORK IT, GIRL! PROFILE OF KIMBERLA LAWSON ROBY

Kimberla Lawson Roby's literary journey started when she self-published her first novel, *Behind Closed Doors,* and has led her to the *New York Times' Bestsellers'* list. Many of her fans say they enjoy the fact that she chooses to deal with real issues in each novel. Those topics include: domestic violence, corruption within the church, weight issues and racial and gender discrimination. Her great success with readers allowed her to leave her 9 to 5 and work from her home in Illinois. It is there that she crafts the characters and storylines for books like *Love and Lies.* The authors of *Work It, Girl!* caught up with this busy and successful writer to gain advice and insight for our readers who desire to work from home.

SIX QUESTIONS FOR KIM ROBY:

1) **WIG:** Did you find it challenging or creatively freeing when you left the traditional work environment to be a full-time home-based writer?

Kim Roby: *Leaving the traditional work environment has been a truly amazing experience. Being a full-time writer, working from my home office and even other locales is in two words, very refreshing. Today, I can't imagine what it would be like if I wasn't able to work on my own terms and do the kind of job that makes me happy.*

2) **WIG:** How do you separate yourself from the common distractions one often encounters when working from home?

Kim Roby: *I must admit that this has been my primary challenge. It seems that there are days when I just can't help wanting to do everything I can think of around the house or I find myself wanting to spend quality time with my husband and before I know it, the* *day is practically over! Then, there is e-mail, e-mail, e-mail. There's also the phone, deliveries, and other distractions, so just recently I've decided that the best way for me to be more disciplined is to rise each morning, Monday through Friday, grab my notebook computer and/or portable word processor and head to a local coffee shop or bookstore to get some uninterrupted work done.*

3) **WIG:** Describe your primary place of work at your home and why it works for you.

Kim Roby: *For the most part, I work from my home office and it's perfect because it's on the lower level and thankfully we live in a subdivision with only twelve houses and the semi-country setting is very quiet and serene. I rarely take my computer onto the main floor, our primary living space, but sometimes I will venture up to the den on the second floor and get lots of writing done. It just sort of depends on how I'm feeling when I'm ready to write the next book.*

4) **WIG:** What do you enjoy most about working from home?

Kim Roby: *I love not having to wake up to an alarm clock and not having to get dressed in a suit and high heels in order to go to work. Our home is a very comfortable and peaceful environment, and I must say that I feel so free and independent. From a career standpoint, working from home is the best feeling in the world.*

5) **WIG:** Please provide tips and advice for women who work from home and need to make the most of this opportunity.

Kim Roby: *Keep your priorities in order in terms of work and in terms of your personal life. In order to be successful with both, you need to have a good balance between those two areas. Follow a daily to-do list and try sticking to set working hours. This isn't always possible, but you should try to make it happen more often than not.*

Network with others in your line of work, specifically those who are where you aspire to be. Read as much about your given industry and learn as much as you possibly can from now on. There will never come a time when you've learned everything there is to know. Remember that professionalism is always key, regardless of what your business or career category might be. Always try to do the right thing. Always treat others the way you want to be treated.

6) **WIG:** In your opinion, what is the difference between "working" and "working it?"

Kim Roby: *"Working" is doing only as much as you have to and settling for less than what God has placed you on this earth to do. "Working it," however, is when you follow your purpose and you do everything you can to be the best that you can be. "Working it" is when you won't accept or offer anything less than excellence.*

The author can be found on the web at www.kimroby.com

CHAPTER 7
Turning Your Hobby into a Career

"Just don't give up trying to do what you really want to do. Where there is love and inspiration, I don't think that you can go wrong."
— Ella Fitzgerald (singer)

As a high school freshman, Theresa Lee was a varsity track captain who wanted to become an Olympic track star. But, her life took a completely different course when she became a teen mom. Over the next few years she experienced many personal trials and tribulations; but, eventually she became a registered nurse. With that accomplishment under her belt, she decided that losing weight was her next goal to conquer. At 5 feet 8 inches tall and 235 pounds, Theresa couldn't seem to win the battle of the bulge. That all changed when she enrolled in an aerobic kickboxing class, and eventually, into a Tae Kwon Do class. It didn't take her long to get hooked on the sport.

"The more I worked out, the more I wanted to work out. I did the 11pm-7am shift at the hospital so I could work out while my kids were at school and planned my other workouts around their activities. I trained about three or four hours a day, every day, and lost 35 pounds in the first month. Five months later I defeated four women in my first tournament."

Today, the nurse-turned-Tae Kwon Do athlete and business owner, earns six figures while pursuing a passion. She competes nationally and internationally, teaches several classes a day, and recently took a group of 14 youth to the U.S. Jr. Olympic Championships. With her own 2500 square foot Michigan studio, she boasts class rolls of about 300 students, and is well-respected in her community. She opened a second Tae Kwon

Do studio and although she sold it to a student, she still is actively involved with testing belts and receives a nominal fee for use of her name for the facility. Theresa, who still works as a full-time registered nurse, has added a travel agency to her studio. The savvy business woman decided to do this because she travels so much and knew it would be smart to pay herself. *"I'm trying to work smarter, not harder,"* she said. Like many people who have parlayed a passion into profit, that simple phrase was once a cliché, but it is now her mantra.

Although Tae Kwon Do was not Theresa Lee's hobby, once she started it, she pursued it with every bit of vigor and excitement that many hobbyists pursue their passions. She studied it. She practiced it. She found satisfaction in it. She LOVED it. If you have an interest that generates even half that enthusiasm and dedication, then you might be able to turn that pastime into a paycheck.

Have you read every book you could find about your hobby? Have you taken classes or do you watch "how-to" television shows to improve your hobby skills? Do family and friends swear you could perform your hobby in your sleep because you talk about it every chance you get, whether anyone wants to listen or not? Are there few things that give you more satisfaction than your hobby? If you answered 'yes' to any of these questions, then you should consider it a viable business or career move. But wait, before you quit your job, there are a few critical issues you should explore.

First, there is a real possibility that your hobby will no longer be fun once it becomes your livelihood and you *have* to do it. If you freelance your talent, having a day job that pays the bills means having the choice to say 'no' to certain projects. Being able to choose the projects you really like, and being able to decide when taking on the project is most convenient for you, is what makes it "fun" to capitalize on something you do in your free time.

Second, if you change careers to make your hobby your full-time gig, what about the possibility of not earning as much money in this new career because you are not as experienced as you were in your old one?

Third, it can be exciting to occasionally have the opportunity to break up the monotony of your current role at work. However, it is possible to change careers and still end up bored to death at work. Therefore, you need to do some soul searching to find out if you are craving variety in your current career and not an entirely new gig. The key to making this decision lies in testing out the change before you commit to it.

Allow us to introduce you to other options:
- Capitalize on your creativity by selling what you make or do (art and crafts, food, clothes, beauty items, accessories, etc.).
- Turn your expertise into an enterprise by teaching others how to do your hobby. Conduct workshops at the community college continuing education programs, places of worship, civic groups, or at your local city or county recreation department.
- Creatively communicate your hobby to others through writing, photography, illustration, or videography. Trade journals, magazines, and newspapers are a great place to start.
- Explore your hobby to discover potential career opportunities.
- Find jobs that allow you to use your hobby-related skills or use those skills at your current place of employment.

Now realize that at some point, the demand for your goods or services could wind up making you have to devote a huge chunk of time to your hobby. Living and breathing this dream could force you to decide whether you should limit the time and effort you spend on it or if you should just take the plunge, full speed ahead. Be ready to decide whether you want to maintain it as a second career or give up your day job to make it a full-time gig.

Accidental Entrepreneurship, Intentional Success

We realize that not every Sister is looking to making money from her leisure activities, but sometimes it just happens that way.

Divas Uncorked was born from a group of ten successful Sisters who shared a desire to learn more about wines around the world and decided to take turns hosting monthly dinners to educate themselves about it. Over the years their knowledge was greatly expanded and they had a full-fledged venture on their hands. They hosted dinners for hundreds of people and held a one-day women's conference. In addition to those activities, they established important relationships with vintners, somme-liers, and wine educators to create a consortium of business owners who would donate money for scholarships. These collaborations also allowed them to provide opportunities for tapping into and expanding the neglected market of women and minorities.

"We looked in our own backyard for women business owners and for people in the industry who were good, but had not gotten a lot of exposure and invited them to be presenters at our events," said Gert Cowan, a member of the Boston-based, Divas Uncorked. *"We also looked for oppor-tunities to mentor students who might be faced with dining with clients and helped them become more savvy about wine."* The group has been written about in magazines and newspapers, has appeared on television shows, is writing a book and now has its own private label, "Divas Uncorked Chardonnay" (Mendocino Wine Company).

"Just when we think 'wow,' something else comes along. But, we make sure that we don't get too caught up in the excitement of it all and forget that our main goal was to getting together with friends and educating ourselves about wines. When we sometimes start to push that back, because we are caught up in the excitement, we have to forget the hype and get rooted in order to go forward again."

The Smart Moves

Turning your hobby into a career only takes a few smart moves if you have the right mindset. This transition needs to have a methodical and logical approach. We recommend that you consider the following options to help you take the slow road to building a hobby-related career:

Use your hobby-related skill in your current job. If you have a hobby that you are good at, convincing your current employer to let you use it is one of the least risky ways to explore that interest. For example, if you work in an office setting and love tinkering with computers although your job doesn't call for it, discuss the interest with your boss. Keep your eyes and ears open for opportunities for you to get involved in computer-related projects. Or, when the office computers just aren't doing what they should, you could come to the rescue. It won't take much to become the 'go-to' person for troubleshooting them and when you decide to apply for an internal position your case may be already made.

Find people who will pay you to provide a service. In some cases, your skills from your hobby won't match your employer's needs. Or you may opt not to worry about conflicts that could arise if you assume two different roles on your job. You may even feel that it wouldn't be advantageous to you to work two different jobs for one salary. If those are real concerns for you, be willing to look outside of your current job. Many businesses and individuals use outsiders on an 'as-needed' basis to save money and time. For example, if you love working with numbers, perhaps you could seek out clients who would pay for bookkeeping services or apply to teach budgeting courses at the local adult education center through a community college.

Get involved with hobby-related organizations to uncover potential jobs. Being in contact with many other people who love what you love is a great way to find out about new ways to use your skills, job opportunities that involve those skills, and people who need your expertise.

Use your skills to transition into a new job. Investigate job vacancies at organizations that provide services or equipment to support your hobby. Your strategy would be to apply for the jobs that fall within your current professional skill set. Then, once you have proven yourself, you can move around within your new company.

If, at this point, all you need is guidance and support to feed your fun-loving soul and your wallet, there are resources out there to direct your path. Various organizations will help you tap into the resources available for you to start a small business (www.sba.org), run a home-based business or make a little extra money "on the side." There are opportunities for you to share your hobby with others. Now go ahead and *work it, girl* because sometimes it's not all about the money!

WORK IT, GIRL! TO-DO LIST

✔ **Develop a marketing tool.** Assuming you have solid experience to demonstrate your capability, decide what will be the right marketing tool to sell yourself to potential employers. Will you write a resume, compose a professional biography, or design a flyer? Study vacancy announcements to determine whether your marketing tool hits the mark with respect to the skills sought out by employers. Craft a cover letter that will describe your transition goal and your background. Don't forget to sell the "soft" skills and the transferable ones that are always an added bonus to employers.

✔ **Prepare for interviews.** Decide what might be the hard questions and practice your responses after jotting down the points you want to make with each one. Since you are changing careers it is safe to assume that the interviewer will be curious about your motives and doubtful about your commitment. How will you answer the questions: Why would you give up all that seniority for a job like this? How sure are you that you will stick to this new area of interest? Why should we hire you?

✔ **Don't have too much fun.** There are two sides to this story—the passion and the profit. Fun is good. It is at least part of the reason you decided to cash in on your passion. Just make sure that you take your new job as seriously as you would any other job in your former career field because now, your hobby is also your livelihood. And by the way, you *will* need to find a new hobby to replace the one that just became your job.

Turning Your Hobby into a Career

When turning your hobby into a career you have to assess the situation. This action planner is an assessment tool that allows you to think it through.

What is your hobby that you can turn into a career? _____

Who will be your clientele? _____

_____

How many hours per day or week are you willing to devote to this career?

_____

_____

_____

What is your desired income from your work?

_____

What is your plan for getting maximum exposure for what you are doing?

_____

_____

_____

_____

List three people who can assist you in making this work.

1) _____

2) _____

3) _____

If you plan to pursue your "hobby to career" dream while still working in another career field, what if anything, is your criteria for quitting that job to devote all of your energy to your hobby?

_____

_____

_____

_____

Why do you love this hobby enough to turn it into a career?

_____

_____

_____

_____

Remember to THINK IT THROUGH!

WORK IT, GIRL! PROFILE OF LISA PRICE

For Lisa Price it was a love of perfume and her desire to spread "good scents" that motivated her to turn her hobby into a career. It all started with mixing potions in the kitchen of her Brooklyn, New York home and evolved into the mega-successful company, Carol's Daughter, Inc. Along the way, the natural beauty products garnered national press and a star-studded client list. The company has designed baskets for A-List celebrities that include Halle Berry and Oprah Winfrey. Price can now count entertainment powerbrokers Will and Jada Pinkett Smith and Jay-Z among her investors. She details her journey from hobby to career in her book *Success Never Smelled So Sweet* and shared her business savvy with the authors of *Work It, Girl!*

Six Questions For Lisa Price:

1) **WIG:** When did you realize that you could turn your kitchen-based hobby, making creams and potions, into a career?

Lisa Price: *It was in August of 1993. I started at my first flea market in May of 1993 and I continued to do flea markets and so forth all summer long. One afternoon in August I was watching Oprah and she had women who had started businesses with little or no money. Listening to these women talk about demographics and marketing, passion and dedication, and loving what you do, I realized that I had a business and it was no longer just my hobby.*

2) **WIG:** What advice do you have for women who are interested in testing the waters to see if their hobby can become a career?

Lisa Price: *Do not give up your regular job until you absolutely have to. It is hard to know just from looking on paper whether or not you can handle the rigors of entrepreneurship and whether or not your business can be successful. Businesses have cycles. Sometimes they are up and sometimes they are down and you have to ride out the tough times.*

3) **WIG:** Celebrities have really embraced your company. What advice can you give to "Sister entrepreneurs" who are trying to gain maximum exposure for their products and/or services?

Lisa Price: *This is hard for me to answer because I was in a unique situation in the beginning given the fact that I worked in television and film production prior to doing this business. This gave me the opportunity to get my products into the hands of hair stylists and make-up artists and also celebrities. The only cost to me was giving up free product in small quantities. I would not suggest someone with no resources send out packages to people or magazines, etc. without knowing whether or not they were received and by whom. The best thing to do is when the opportunity comes to you, seize it.*

Also, think small. Every year at my boys' schools we give out Carol's Daughter products as gifts to teachers and students. The students take it home and their parents use it. My husband is also "Santa" at his job. From this our business has gotten numerous customers that purchased more than once. You may find yourself one year giving out ten gifts and then the following year getting ten orders.

4) **WIG:** Why is it important to follow your spirit?

Lisa Price: *It is important to follow your spirit because it is never wrong.*

5) **WIG:** What brings you the most satisfaction professionally?

Lisa Price: *Making changes and making a difference. I have gotten so much from being a part of the business on a personal and spiritual level that it far surpasses any monetary gain. I am a stronger person. I have wonderful relationships with people I would not have otherwise met. I can say that I have helped to make a change in this world for African-American women and the beauty industry.*

6) **WIG:** What, in your opinion, is the difference between "working" and "working it?"

Lisa Price: *The difference is the difference between doing a job and having that job work for you. I work hard and put in a lot of hours and never finish what I have to do each day. But it's okay, because it's my choice to do it and there's love in that.*

For information on Lisa Price's company visit her online at www.carols-daughter.com.

CHAPTER 8
When It's Not ALL About the Money

"Once you understand what your work is and you do not try to avert your eyes from it, but attempt to invest energy in getting that work done, the universe will send you what you need.
— Toni Cade Bambara (author)

A number of years ago, Denyne Anderson was a single parent raising two girls on her own and working as the vice president of a bank in Des Moines, Iowa. She had a six-figure salary and received bonuses of $10,000-$20,000 a year, but she was miserable surrounded by a "profit over humanity mentality." Ultimately, she quit her job. And despite everyone thinking she was crazy, she went back to school to get a master's degree in divinity. She and is now the executive director of a national organization that helps poor women and their children secure housing, acquire training and obtain jobs.

Denyne had discovered, like many more people are discovering these days, that it's not all about the money. Countless surveys and reports are showing that regardless of how long workers have been in the game, they are buying into this concept. Case in point, CNN Money cites the Undergraduate Ideal Employer Ranking Survey by Universum Communications (May 2006). The poll by of more than 37,000 students from 207 schools in the U.S. shows that "students would rather have a good health plan than a high salary." It further cites that "most college students said their career goals are to balance their personal and professional life, pursue further education, build a sound financial base and contribute to society." Now some of you may be thinking, "it's easy for them to say that when they are young, inexperienced, and don't have to support a family." And that may be true, but "middlers" are sharing the same sentiments.

If you are beginning to approach middle age it is likely that your lifestyle, financial commitments and outlook have changed since you were in your early twenties. Now you are probably more concerned with balancing family, work, and community. You may also be figuring out how to save for your children's college tuition and your retirement, not to mention struggling with career or job satisfaction. Do you need a job or career change that will help you better align your goals in these areas? Are you tired of feeling unsatisfied no matter what you achieve at work? Do you find helping others rewarding? Like LaToya Bates, have you realized that when it comes to having a satisfying job it's not all about the money?

LaToya has a background that makes her capable of running any private or public social service agency around. Or, she could establish a lucrative private practice. However, the licensed and certified social worker and manager of respite programming with a master's degree in social service administration believes that either of those opportunities would be time consuming and emotionally draining.

"My twins are only five years old and it is important that I am there for them. My family means more to me than my career ever will. As a social worker I am keenly aware of the importance of quality time with family and the long term affects the bonding can have on the children," she said. *"One of the best things about my current position is the flexibility. I work from home two days a week. I am not dealing with the commute to and from Washington, D.C. and getting the children to and from school is a less stressful event. It also allows me to participate in extracurricular events for the children."* It seems that LaToya has discovered far more than money.

Finally, if you are beginning to think about retirement, think about how you would like to spend your time. Will you be happy that you will have the freedom to react to you whims? Will you want to start a second career? If so, then you might also be interested in what an employer can offer you in the way of non-financial rewards.

In today's society the "bling-bling" mentality is prevalent throughout the media. Contemporary songs, movies and books are filled with references to designer clothes, expensive champagne and homes in the Hamptons. Yet, some Sisters are happy without big bank. You can be too! Now don't misunderstand us. By no means are we "anti-money" or advocating working for less than you are worth. We just want to encourage you to follow your spirit and your heart to job and career satisfaction because the money chase doesn't always end in happiness.

Will you ditch your current job in favor of a more service-oriented position? Will your decision to help others require that you leave your current employer? Let's explore some options.

There are a lot of people and causes in the world that need your help. These opportunities provide you with a sense doing something that matters and making a difference in the life of others. Some of those careers include teaching, social work, counseling, nursing and work in the non-profit sector. These positions, also known as jobs in the "helping profession," don't bring in big bank. However, a lot of Sisters who work in them feel like they have hit the jackpot.

Teaching is an excellent example. A recent report from the NEA Research Department (Teacher Pay 1940 – 2000: Losing Ground, Losing Status), which is based on US census data, finds that annual pay for teachers has fallen sharply over the past 60 years in relation to the annual pay of other workers with college degrees. The report states that, "Throughout the nation the average earnings of workers with at least four years of college are now over 50 percent higher than the average earnings of a teacher."

First grade teacher Saundra Dore acknowledges that teachers are underpaid and sometimes unappreciated but she truly loves her work. She agrees that true job satisfaction is not about the money. *"I just feel that teaching is my purpose and that's why I was put on this earth," she said.* She has spent over twenty years in the classroom and hasn't been lured away by a higher paying job in administration, even after earning a master's degree. *"I belong here. First grade is when you shape them and mold them and I love it!"*

Many of the children she teaches at St. Helena Early Learning Center come from disadvantaged backgrounds and although she received other job offers in more affluent areas she made the choice to be of service in that community. The married mother of two said that it has to be about more than a paycheck because it comes with challenges. *"Teaching takes a tremendous amount of time but what makes the time OK is when you are really doing it from your heart."* Since 1984 Dore has followed her heart and each year she said it brings her back to the classroom because, for her, is like a rebirth.

"I still love it because it makes me grow as a person."

If you can imagine yourself helping others, forget about money for a minute and think about the possibilities.

- ❖ Whom or what do you want to help? Children? Families? Couples? Elderly? Animals? The environment?
- ❖ How do you want to help? Do you want to teach? Counsel? Provide health care? Research?
- ❖ Where can you provide this help? Schools? Non-profit organizations? Hospitals?

If you are really not sure what you want to do, then we suggest that you begin by volunteering to get a first-hand view of these types of jobs. Figure out which organizations in your local community have the types of volunteer experiences you seek. Then contact the staff to find out the application process and proceed with it using the same strategies you would if you were seeking paid employment. Arrange an informational interview, if possible, so you can have the chance to share your background and areas of interest with the hiring manager. At the same time, be prepared to ask questions about the organization and how it works. To make the best impression, you might consider dressing as if you were going on an interview for a paid position. After all, you may wind up discovering a paid position for which you want to apply because first impressions are lasting.

Visit more than one place so that you can make comparisons and conduct a more thorough analysis of your potential satisfaction with each of them. There are web-based volunteer opportunity databases you may find helpful. Try www.volunteer.org/nz for the Global Volunteer network, which offers opportunities in community projects throughout the world in developing countries. Volunteer.gov/gov Web Portal connects people with public sector volunteer opportunities. Teach for America (www.teachforamerica.org) recruits recent college graduates to teach for two years in under-sourced urban or rural public schools, but welcomes all levels of experience. Volunteermatch.com allows you to plug in your own criteria for local volunteering.

And now, let's get back to the money question. Although we believe that it's not all about the money, we don't encourage you to be a martyr when it comes to your paycheck. Instead, take action to tip the scales in your financial favor.

Look for alternatives to accepting pay that is considerably lower than your current salary or not enough to make ends meet. For instance, perhaps you may need to consider transferring your current skill set into an organization whose mission is focused on "making a difference." For example, an environmental company, and seek paid employment there. Another alternative is to seek out opportunities to participate in existing community programs in which your current employer is involved or volunteer to start one for your employer.

Determine what non-financial rewards could make up the difference in what salary you would like and the one employers are offering. Will there be training and development opportunities or tuition reimbursement for college courses? Successful completion of these might later lead to a pay raise or promotion. Could you use more time with your family or time to pursue other interests (including freelance work)? Then an alternative work schedule could do the trick. See Chapter 5, "Staying Put: Achieving Success without Making a Move," and Chapter 6, "Make

Working from Home Work for You." Can you negotiate more vacation or sick time? What about better or more pension and stock options?

Make strategic financial changes. Give yourself time to get ahead before switching to a lower paying job. Moves like paying down credit card debt, refinancing your mortgage, consolidating your bills and increasing your savings can make a big difference in your ability to adapt to lower pay. Prepare for a lower level of spending. Create a budget up front that will help you stay within your new constraints. Figure out where you waste the most money and plan to cut those costs. Set goals for saving and then reward yourself for reaching them.

Sometimes it may not be all about the money. That's something you'll have to decide for yourself. Maybe the only way to find out what it is really all about is, perhaps, to go out on a limb and explore all the possibilities.

WORK IT, GIRL! TO-DO LIST

✔ **Create a bliss list.** Jobs that bring you satisfaction can put you in a professional state of bliss. If bliss is defined as a state of great happiness and joy, make a list detailing what it is about your current job that makes you feel that way. If you can't think of anything, you may not be where you need to be to experience happiness. If you list is long, you may want to stick around and enjoy the ride!

✔ **Take inventory of your possessions.** If you are unhappy with your job but stay in it to continue to buy $400 purses and sit pretty in the latest Benz, you have to know you can't buy happiness. If you could, your possessions would be making you happy. Maybe it's time to consider a less expensive, but quality, purse and driving a used Benz that is in mint condition. We believe that happiness is one of the greatest things you can possess.

✔ **Ask for her testimony.** If you see a Sister who is always smiling and happy in her career you should seek her out and ask what makes her so happy with where she is professionally. We are not saying that the money won't be a part of her elation because money adds a level of security and peace. However, we are confident that it won't be the only reason this Sister has a smile on her face. Money is great but it's not all about the money!

When It's Not ALL About the Money

This chapter is more about determining if you are happy at work than it is about your salary. It's about determining if your current J-O-B is where you need to be. Are you happy at work?

1) On a scale of 1-10, rate your overall job satisfaction. (10=Extremely Happy) _____

2) How does your work make you feel inside?

_____

_____

_____

3) What do you enjoy most about your career?

_____

_____

4) Are you active in your profession outside of your job requirements? For example, are you involved in professional organizations and/or volunteer in your field beyond your work hours?

_____

_____

_____

5) List the three people that you admire most professionally? Are they in your field?

_____   _____

_____   _____

_____   _____

6) Has the stress of your job or work environment ever led to health complications for you? _____

7) Would you still be at your job if you could get another one? _____

8) If you could afford to work for free, but still desired to work, would you remain in your current job?_____

9) Is money your primary reward in your career? _____

10) If it's not "all" about the money in your career, what is it all about for you?

_____

_____

_____

WORK IT, GIRL! PROFILE OF CHERYL BROUSSARD

Cheryl Broussard is on a mission to inspire and empower wealth to people through financial education. She is a registered investment advisor, money coach and CEO of Cheryl Broussard & Co., Inc. Her California-based financial firm offers consulting, training and personal financial advice. Her bestselling books, including *Sister CEO* and *The Black Woman's Guide to Financial Independence,* are just a part of what makes her a sought-after money expert. The authors of *Work It, Girl!* sought her out to provide our readers with sound advice about work and money.

Six Questions for Cheryl Broussard:

1) **WIG:** What would you say to encourage a woman who's torn between a high paying job that doesn't make her happy and a position that may bring more satisfaction but less money?

Cheryl Broussard: *Go for the position that will bring more satisfaction and less money. Your career takes up a major part of your life so you don't want that time spent in unhappiness. As a matter of fact, working in a job you don't like actually will cost you more money in the long run because oftentimes we use shopping as a coping technique to deal with our unhappiness on the job. We shop, get deeper in debt, become more unhappy, shop some more and the cycle continues. Many studies have proven that happiness in a career or a business is the primary reason a person became financially successful, not the other way around. So find work that will make you happy, stick with it and you'll see that more money will come.*

2) **WIG:** You have said that you don't have to be rich to have financial freedom. Please explain.

Cheryl Broussard: *Many women believe that they must be a million-aire in order to have financial freedom. Therefore, they are always chasing the millionaire carrot. Of course if they don't become a millionaire they become disappointed and discouraged. They end up not handling their money to the best of their ability. Well, you don't need to be rich or a millionaire to have financial freedom. It really depends on the type of lifestyle you want to live. You can make $30,000 a year and have financial freedom as long as your monthly expenses are low and you have no credit card debt. The definition of financial freedom is different for everyone, but for me it means I have consistent passive income (passive means I don't have to work at it to make the money) coming in every month to pay all my monthly expenses and have money to save and invest.*

3) **WIG**: What do you believe is the biggest money myth?

Cheryl Broussard: *Making more money will eliminate all your money problems. This is so far from the truth. Most of our money chal-lenges are from our bad habits with managing money. It is really quite easy to make money; the tough part is keeping it. It is extremely important that we change our mindset about money and that we become more disciplined and develop better habits with mastering our money. We need to keep track of the outflow and inflow of our money daily. We need to read our statement every month so we know how much we are charging on our credit cards. We need to balance our checking account. What I'm talking about here is that we must become much more conscious of what we do with our money in order for us to really master money.*

4) **WIG**: What do you find most rewarding about helping women take charge of their money, build wealth and achieve financial security?

Cheryl Broussard: *For the last 23 years I have been on a mission to educate women of color about money. Initially, I didn't think anyone really cared or was listening. But, that was never the case.*

I have received letters and e-mails from women saying how they read my books or heard me speak and followed my step-by-step advice and now they are completely out of debt, they bought a new home and they are making $10,000 a month in their new business. This is outstanding and it is a great feeling knowing that you are changing people's lives and you are helping them to fulfill their dreams. I believe that is really why we are here on this earth. It's not just about amassing a whole bunch of material stuff, but really about helping and supporting each other. Look at Oprah. She's a billionaire and could stop working and simply lay on the beach all day and do nothing, yet she is out there serving others.

5) **WIG**: What are the keys to living well financially, regardless of your income?

Cheryl Broussard: *The key is managing your money and developing habits to save and grow your money. You want your money to work for you, not you work for your money. You want to focus on building assets that will provide you with positive passive cash flow. Some examples are real estate, a business, savings and investments like mutual funds. These types of investments work 24/7 without your involvement. Another reason you want to build your wealth is so you can pass it on to future generations. African-American families have the lowest net worth in this country and the primary reason is due to lack of owning a home/real estate. Real estate is the number one appreciating asset out there I encourage families to buy their own home and to buy a home for each of their children, so when they are of age they will already own a home. The impact of doing this one thing in the Black community would be phenomenal. Our children would not have to start from ground zero and we would be able to continue to pass down the wealth to several generations. The other thing that is important is that we must maintain good credit. Pay your bills on time, don't take on more debt than you need and monitor your credit report annually*

138

for any mistakes. Your credit will help you to leverage your dollars to grow your wealth.

6) **WIG:** What, in your opinion, is the difference between "working" and "working it"?

Cheryl Broussard: *"Working" means nothing can happen unless you are involved in it. This is what I talked about earlier when I said you want your money to work for you. "Working it" means your money is making money. So when you invest $1 and get back $2, you have worked it and doubled your money. You can work your money in a regular savings account at your bank or credit union. You can "work it" in real estate. You can "work it" in the stock market. The key is that you must stop spending it on stuff you don't need and invest it so it can compound and grow.*

For more information visit her company online at
www.cherylbroussard.com.

CHAPTER 9
Out on a Limb: Excelling in Daring and Non-Traditional Careers

"My mother told me that I was capable of doing anything. 'Be ambitious,' she said, 'Jump at de sun.'"
— Zora Neale Hurston (writer)

As a child, April Weeden-Washington thought that she would be a doctor or psychologist. Later, when she went to college, she majored in public relations. While working as a casting agent in the movie industry she hired stunt coordinator William Washington. Not only did she end up marrying William, she also jumped into a whole new world.

April became so enthralled with stunt work and was surprised at how much she could do. She felt this way even though she had strength and endurance training from 25 years of ballet training. It wasn't long before she was spending her days performing death defying feats that are a part of most people's nightmares: riding the tops of speeding trains, falling off running horses, jumping out of moving cars and plunging down elevator shafts. She made $30,000 in her first year and by the 7th year she was raking in a six-figure salary.

Today, April has become one of the most highly sought-after Black stuntwomen. Her resume boasts work on more than 300 major feature films and television shows. They include: *Thin Line between Love and Hate, Eraser, Anaconda, Why do Fools Fall in Love, Blade, I Still Know What You Did Last Summer, Hot Boyz, Swordfish* and *Minority Report.* Her TV work *includes Strong Medicine, Buffy the Vampire Slayer,* and *JAG.* April also coordinates stunts and co-owns, with her husband, a production company, ranch and boarding stable in California. The wife and mother of one also won first place in the National Barrel Horse Association's 4D Division competition in barrel racing. The daring move to enter this career field just felt natural to April and she didn't let *anything* hold her back. *"People said it couldn't be done, but my new career took off so fast that I didn't worry about what they were saying. I had a slight fear of the unknown when I left behind a life that revolved around dancing since I was three years old, but my faith in God and a wonderful family provided a support system."*

You want to be a *WHAT*?! All your life you have dreamed about crashing through windows from waaaaay up high, diving out of buildings engulfed by flames, putting the pedal to the metal and burning rubber at over 100 miles per hour, or chasing down criminals in back alleys. But in real life, you don't dare pursue those dreams. Instead, you go to a more conventional job, earn a decent living and return home at the end of the day to live vicariously through others who gets to live your dreams. But, you now realize that's not enough.

Why aren't more women going out on a limb and pursuing careers that may be daring or non-traditional? We think that although everyone has their own story, these are some reasons that Sisters are not taking the leap!

FEAR OF FAILURE: Fear can stop us in our tracks every time we attempt to do something big! Much of that fear is rooted in what we believe will happen if we fail. However, we need to concentrate on what will happen when we succeed. It really is unfortunate to be haunted by the knowledge that because we didn't try, we will never know if we could make it to the top. Fear must be confronted. Just Do It!

COMFORT ZONE: Some of us are unwilling to do anything that will cause the least bit of discomfort. Any goal that is physical in nature will require you to push yourself. You may not be the first female to train a heavy-weight boxer to the coveted belt if you aren't working out with the bag yourself. A fear of not speaking up because you are not comfortable doing it will not allow for the self-promotion that you often need to show others that you are knowledgeable enough to move to the next level or position. Step up. Walk out on faith.

NO SOURCE OF INSPIRATION: Motivation is often tied to something tangible or intangible that we can set our mind on and that propels us further. It could be the words from a father who is no longer with you or a pen that you have purchased for your first book signing despite the fact that you haven't even written the first word. There are many sources for inspiration in our professional lives we just have to keep them active in our hearts and minds.

LACK OF A CONCRETE MODEL: Life can't be just about modeling what others have done in the past. If you are in a quest to be the first female president of the United States there is no one before you. You would make history and set the standard. Stop looking for a blueprint and become the model others can follow.

READING THE SCRIPT YOU ARE GIVEN: For many women it is simply time to "flip the script" or write a new one. Some of us go through life as if our life is pre-scripted and we have to get all our lines right. Well change that frame of thought and recognize that you are the director and if you are not happy with a scene, you can say CUT. Most of these scripts contain content that is shaped more by family, friends, history, fear and other things that make us feel that we can't ad lib in our lives. We say, either make edits to your life script or skip the rewrites and start from scratch.

"Don't be afraid to step out on faith and try it. Whatever it is you think you want to do, try it. If it doesn't work, then try something else; but, just don't stop trying until you find out what works for you. You will never get there if you don't even try," said April. She cherishes the fact that she has not only has realized great success, but has also been able to give back to others by helping them do well in the industry.

There is no greater motivation for us than someone who has walked the walk and continues to do so. We are fortunate to have countless role models who can motivate us, as only Black women can, to take on the world and conquer the career fields thought not to be an option for us. There is Effa Manley, whose business savvy as co-owner of the Negro League's Newark Eagles earned her the recognition of becoming the first woman elected into the Baseball Hall of Fame (2006); Condoleeza Rice, the first Black female Secretary of State (2005); Rikkia "Lady Racer" Mills, the first Black Woman professional drag car racer (2002); Mae Jemison, astronaut and the first Black woman in space; Sharon Pratt Dixon, the first Black woman to serve as mayor of a major city (DC); Rosemary Cloud, believed to be the first Black female fire chief in the nation; and Oprah, the first Black woman to own her own television production company. The list goes on and on and on. Sisters, we have history. These women dared to take the plunge and you should too!

Woman's Work?

Non-traditional occupations for women are defined by the U.S. Department of Labor to be any jobs in which women comprise 25% or less of the total employed. These jobs include office machine repairers, construction and building inspectors, railroad conductors, machinists, truck drivers, fire fighters, aircraft pilots, construction occupations, and small engine mechanics. Unfortunately, there is still the misconception that certain jobs are men's work. Women who *work it* in careers that are traditionally dominated by men often experience daily prejudices from their male counterparts.

Shawn Craig-Parker, a project manager for a major communications company in the Pennsylvania, agreed to share a series of real life scenarios that happened to her.

"For my first job, I was offered two jobs at the same time, with the same company. Initially, I thought the engineering job in a cushy Maryland office was clearly the best choice. After some consideration, I took the construction job to see what a turbine looks like, to touch a condenser, to really see the items I'd only studied in books. So, I found myself on a

construction site in Providence, Rhode Island, many miles from (my home-town) South Carolina.

"With nine years under my belt, I manage 23 people—mostly men. The road to my current position was not easy. As a woman in a non-traditional field, I am questioned constantly and it is always a struggle to prove my abilities where with a more 'stereotypical' engineer, the capabilities are assumed.

"I have been in meetings with all levels of employees where inappropriate things were said by educated people. The stereotypes are so ingrained that they don't even realize what they are saying. They should know better, even if it's only for legal reasons. I was transferring two people to another group—one male and one female. My manager strongly suggested that I give the male a raise prior to moving him. When I questioned him 'why', my manager stammered. He had no reasons. They were equal in most respects. It hadn't dawned on him that he was discriminating.

"Recently, I was interviewed by the top engineering manager in our office for a higher level position. After the meeting, he told others that he "loved" me but he didn't know if I would be respected enough in the position because I am a woman. I was shocked that a man in his position didn't realize that he was discriminating. Based on his comments, I knew he would sit idle if I was ever disrespected. He wasn't going to be the one who would demand a tolerant and respectful work culture.

"As a woman in a non-traditional industry, it can be tough to balance the feminine side and to not feel that it has to be suppressed. I feel self-conscious going to work in a skirt or with a new hairdo. I pumped breast milk for over a year for both of my kids. After they were 6 months old and I was still making my treks to the pumping room, I felt judged by my colleagues. It was so important to provide my babies with the best possible nutrition that I pressed forward despite the looks and the comments behind my back."

Women in non-traditional jobs experience daily prejudices from customers, too.

"There have been plenty of times when train riders assume that the male employees are the conductors because conductors are in charge of the entire train and its crew," said Patricia Edwards-Ussery who was the senior Black conductor on a Boston metropolitan area commuter rail, before relocating to Baltimore. *"I see it over and over again. When passengers are told something, with which they disagree, they express wanting to 'see the conductor'. They won't believe what I tell them. But, a male could say the exact same thing and they will believe him, even if he is my assistant conductor. However, I don't let myself get wrapped around all that. I have been with this company for 14 years, so I just follow the guidelines that are written in the Service Standards Manual for Train Service and move on with my job."*

Some women in non-traditional careers have reported feelings of isolation/loneliness and sexual harassment, so the authors recommend that you educate yourself about prevention, legal recourse, and available support systems. We also recommend that you don't let it get you down.

"I do like the camaraderie of other women, but I don't have many women peers; therefore, I seek out women in other groups for friendships. My male peers have taken this as a slight," said Shawn.

So what are the benefits to being in a career that is non-traditional for women? For starters, jobs that are traditionally held by men pay more; offer great benefits, especially when in unionized fields; and have better potential for advancement based upon established career progression models. According to Non-traditional Employment for Women, a nonprofit organization that trains women for skilled jobs in blue-collar industries, over half of the most common trades in New York City's construction industry pay more than $20 per hour. For single mothers, a job with a pay check that can more than support her family, provide health benefits for her children, and allow her to meet her financial goals is a gold mine. For other Sisters who want to be financial contributors in their households, these dollars can go a long way.

Is non-traditional employment for you? To learn about self-assessment tools and have access to several types of them log on to Www.work4women.org/about/assessment.cfm.

If you choose to go the road less traveled by women, your plan should be to do whatever it takes to be at the top of your game.

Maryum Ali, daughter of Muhammad Ali, wasn't at all surprised when her sister Laila decided to pursue a field that is dominated by men. *"When she told me she wanted to box, I told her that I knew she would be successful. When Laila puts her mind to something she is incredibly focused. She was smart enough to train like a champion has to train."*

April Weeden-Washington agrees that training is vital to success in daring and non-traditional careers. When asked what advice she would give her daughter if she were seeking the same, she said, *"Whatever profession you choose, know what you are doing. Be over-prepared. Be qualified. Be trained. Continue to train."*

Shawn believes that helping children navigate through career choices can be a challenge. *"The advice is no longer, 'Go to college and get a good job.' I will tell my children to pursue their passion despite what society tells them. I hope to help them find and focus on the activity that makes their heart sing. As a parent who wants to protect my children, it can be difficult to not taint them because of my preconceived notions. I often think about successful rapper and actor Will Smith. He turned down a scholarship to the prestigious Massachusetts Institute of Technology (MIT) to pursue music. I can imagine that his parents must have speculated about that choice, but look at the outcome. Will Smith could have been one of the engineers I see every day. Those who are 'stuck' in engineering jobs despite their true desires. I hope to give my kids the love and support they need to truly find their purpose."*

Join us in changing society's views on what Sisters can and cannot do and in encouraging the next generation to do the same!

In a *Jet* magazine interview Rikkia Mills, the first Black female professional drag car racer for the national Hot Rod Association, said *"It doesn't make a difference what nationality I am, because the fact that I'm*

147

a girl just drives them (her male counterparts) *nuts, more so than* (my) *being Black."*

WORK IT, GIRL! TO-DO LIST

✔ **Study the Story.** Women who are celebrated as trailblazers in their fields have stories that are often well-documented due to magazine articles, television profiles and other sources of media archiving. Do your research and learn about how a woman you admire *worked it!*"

✔ **Take the Hands-On Approach.** In the chapter text, Shawn Craig-Parker talked about opting to take a job that would give her more hands on experience in her field. It is an invaluable tool to know how what you want to do really works. You may be a great industrial manager who supervises production workers, but to be really knowledgeable you need to know how to operate the machinery. Be as actively involved as you can to gain more knowledge of what you ultimately want to do.

✔ **Use Your Imagination.** Gospel superstar Kirk Franklin has an inspiring song titled, "Imagine." Lyrically he states, "This song is dedicated to people like me, those that struggle with insecurities, acceptance and even self-esteem, you never felt pretty enough, you never felt good enough, but imagine God whispering in your ear telling you it's all gone." If you can't imagine yourself in a particular role, how will it ever happen? Work on your insecurities and doubts and imagine yourself where you want to be.

Out on a Limb: Excelling in Daring and Non-Traditional Careers

One of the things our research and personal interviews for this chapter produced was the knowledge that women who excel in this way step outside of what they have been told, what they have seen and what others feel. Let this Action Planner inspire you to listen to your heart, believe beyond what you may see and feel that you can do it!

Remember why you do it. Many of us have known what we wanted to be since childhood, while others figured it out later in life. Reignite you passion by writing down why you want to do this:

_____

_____

_____

_____

HE/SHE/THEY SAY. Make a list of all the reasons that you will hear or have already heard that, if not checked, can taint your *success.*

_____

_____

_____

_____

I SAY. I can be successful because _____

_____

_____

_____

Speak Their Names. Women's lives are greatly impacted by other women. Who are the women in your life who can provide you with the emotional support that you will need on your journey?

_____   _____

_____   _____

Who Are You? To be *non-traditional* and *daring* you have to have a strong sense of self. Use the following space to answer the all important question: "Who Am I?"

_____

_____

_____

_____

_____

_____

_____

WORK IT, GIRL! PROFILE OF MICHELE JONES

Michele S. Jones is the first woman in U.S. history to serve as command sergeant major in the U.S. Army Reserve. She explains to *Work It, Girl!* readers why she serves, answers the authors' six questions and provides Key Notes with useful advice. Editorial Note: The U.S. Army prefers capitalization of the following words: Soldier and Family (when referring to those of Soldiers).

Six Questions for CSM Michele Jones:

CSM Michele Jones: *"First, I would be remiss if I did not share why I chose to serve in the Army. I do not have a job but have a passion for what I do. Most importantly, I believe in what I do and yes I <u>am</u> willing to die for those things that I believe in. The three things that I believe in and am willing to die for are God, country and family—in that order. God because he gave me life. My country because it is my way of life. My family because they are my life. Serving as a Soldier is the only job in the world that protects those three things. On that note, I serve as a Soldier to ensure that all American female citizens and those that benefit and are protected by the laws of this country, can choose to have a career, choose their life's path and excel in a country where women are afforded the same rights as a man."*

1) **WIG**: Many women don't consider military service a viable career option for them, yet you have excelled in the Army. What advice would you give to women who want to excel in areas that are traditionally dominated by men?

CSM Michele Jones: *I ALWAYS KNEW THAT I WANTED TO BE SOLDIER. (Smile) My advice would be:*

1) *Know what you really want.*
2) *If you want it, go for it. Do not listen to the naysayers.*
3) *Just because the field is dominated by men, do not use it as an excuse not to succeed.*
4) *A woman has the right to choose her profession based on desires, passions, and the skill sets she possesses or is pursuing.*
5) *Do your homework and research, know your craft and NEVER use gender as a reason or rationale to get the job or keep it.*
6) *Talk to trusted people in the field, both experienced and inexperienced, ASK THE TOUGH QUESTIONS.*
7) *Stay positive, stay focused and stay on point. DO NOT let negativity stop you from achieving your goals. Instead, use it as a catalyst to propel your forward.*
8) *Learn the whole business, not just your interest. But also, more importantly, the things that you are not interested in. BE THE SUBJECT MATTER expert and the JACK-OF-ALL-TRADES.*
9) *Build your team. Establish your support system, and NEVER EVER forget to thank them!*
10) *Never forget to acknowledge everyone from the custodial staff to the CEO. Have a kind word for all.*

<u>KEY NOTE:</u> *As an woman, when you are introduced or in a meeting for the first time you have about 10 seconds to grab their attention, 30 seconds to keep it, 60 seconds to set yourself up for success — whether you will be heard or tuned out, make it count. Listen to yourself speak. Go to a voice coach if necessary.*

2) **WIG:** How does it feel to make history as the first woman in your position?

CSM Michele Jones: Surreal, even after four years I find that someone who just wanted to be a Soldier, had a belief in her abilities and loved what she did, made history. I still don't believe it. (Smile)

Humbling, that Soldiers, Families, military and many people outside of the military are so proud and treat me like I was their daughter-mother-sister-wife-friend. It is truly humbling, a blessing from God.

Amazing, not because I didn't think I was capable, but considering all the women who have served before me, to be the first one selected is a gift from God. There were others who were definitely qualified, but were not given the opportunity. It never dawned on me that I would make history when I was being considered. All I knew was that I was qualified, would do an exceptional job and give all that I had to the position, Soldiers and Families. I was just a command sergeant major who happened to be a woman.

The fact the Army Reserve had the first female in the top noncommissioned officer position was logical. We have the highest percentage of women in the Army Reserve and in the senior ranks within the Army (Army Reserve, Active Component and the National Guard).

<u>KEY NOTE</u>: *Let what you bring to the table be the reason for your success, not your gender, not your ethnicity.*

3) **WIG:** What keeps you strong when you are faced with challenges and adversity?

CSM Michele Jones: My faith, my Family, my friends and whom I represent. Soldiers and their Families are counting on me to effect change, to be their voice, to represent them and their interests. My feelings, my obstacles, are irrelevant. It was never about me, but about those that I served, "my babies"—my Soldiers. Let's just say I was "Big Momma Army", protecting her children. Like any good mother, you put any and all obstacles, adversity and challenges aside to do what is best for or is in the best interest of your children. The Army is where being a Soldier, a warrior and a leader differs from most organizations—my inability or lack of focus can hurt someone for life. It has a direct impact on every aspect of a Soldier's life and their Family's.

KEY NOTE: *You can never let it be PERSONAL—leave the emotions at the door.*

4) **WIG**: You have joined the ranks of women who have broken barriers in their fields. What women in history have most inspired you?

CSM Michele Jones:
  Josephine Baker— Lived life her way, making her choices, making her decisions and loving her children.
  My mother, Doris H. Jones – The drive to excel, to be a professional and to be a loving wife and mother.
  My grandmother, Fedora Brooks – The love of Family and God, very traditional, very southern.
  My grandmother, Magdalene Harris – The love of travel and the art of flirtation, very non-traditional.
  Condoleeza Rice – never loses her professionalism, a diplomat, and both an official and unofficial ambassador for African-American women throughout the world.

5) **WIG**: What have you found most rewarding about your career?

CSM Michele Jones: That fact that I have represented the finest and most professional group of Soldiers in the world. I have seen and have experienced the passion and commitment of Soldiers. We ask so much of them and their Families—yet they continue to serve. Having been instrumental in the changing of laws, regulations and policies that affect Soldiers and Families has also been rewarding. I have had a direct impact on individuals, both military and civil-

ians, with my leadership philosophy—T-L-C-3 Training, Leadership, Coaching, Counseling and Caring. This means giving them the tools, showing them how to use them and learning from their mistakes. I believe in giving them room to grow and to develop skill sets and values that they can use for life, the Army, the professional world AND their private lives.

6) WIG: What, in your opinion, is the difference between "working" and "working it?"

CSM Michele Jones: "Working" means riding the bull and letting it take you where it wants you to go. It means you being in a reacting state and being passive in your life and its direction. "Working it" means grabbing the bull by the horns and steering it in the direction that you want it to go. Sure, you may get tossed around, get some bumps and bruises and go in the wrong direction for a minute. But, at the end of the day you know you took an active role in the direction that you want to go. And by the way, sooner or later that bull just lays down, you step off it and step over it on your terms! As I progressed in my career I NEVER FORGOT: I am where I am because of my Soldiers. I am who I am because of my Soldiers. It is because of my commitment and responsibility to my Soldiers that I promise today, tomorrow and always to train and take care of Soldiers."

-Command Sergeant Major Michele S. Jones
9th Command Sergeant Major of the Army Reserve
"God, Country and Family I Serve"

CHAPTER 10
The Psychology of Success

Encouraging the Next Generation

*"All that you accomplish or fail to accomplish in life is a direct
result of the images you hold in your mind."*
–Hortense Canady (Past President, Delta Sigma Theta Sorority Inc.)

Prolific singers have stories to tell. They often capture the spirit of a
time and space in their own consciousness or a depiction of what's going
on in the world. Although some artists hide behind the music that others
create for them, others use their instrument to express their deepest
thoughts and beliefs. Singer India Arie's lyrics often champion *"Strength,
Courage and Wisdom,"* her inspirational song title. How delightful it is to
hear her lyrically proclaim *"I am not my hair. I am not this skin. I am the
soul that lives within?"* When we know who we are, at our best and worst,
we can sing a happy song!

Many experts agree that our individual path to success is greatly
impacted by the way we feel about ourselves, our self-esteem.
Psychotherapist Julia Boyd's book, *In the Company of My Sisters: Black
Women and Self-Esteem*, covers the emotional issues and realities of
being a Black woman. In it, she defines self-esteem as "a core of personal
beliefs that we develop about ourselves over the years."

In the text, Boyd recalls that one of her first experiences with self-
esteem was watching the movie "Gone with the Wind." The author read
the book first and pictured herself as the main character, Scarlett.
However, watching the movie changed her belief about her ability to *be*
Scarlett O'Hara.

"As for me, reading "Gone with the Wind" *allowed me to believe I was Scarlett, with all of her lovable charm. Seeing the movie* "Gone with the Wind" *zapped me back into the 'Black reality' of being a small powerless ten-year-old Black girl child. Could I still be lovable if I wasn't White? The personal answer I gave myself was yes!"*

As Boyd's story illustrates, a sense of self-value, or lack of it, develops early in life. It is often impacted by the images that we see and the things that we are told. Given the same set of circumstances, another young girl may have been scarred by the "Gone with the Wind" experience and concluded that she was unworthy of love, respect or esteem. Our conclusions about self-worth impact all aspects of our lives, including our careers.

The Black working woman continues to evolve. In the 1950s, most Black women who worked outside the home worked as maids and in other domestic jobs; therefore, young Black girls tended to imagine themselves in roles like those. We've come a long way baby! That evolution was the subject of the 2003 *Newsweek* cover story "From Schools to Jobs, Black Women Are Rising Much Faster than Black Men: What It Means for Work, Family and Race Relations." The article reported that, "once consigned to only menial work, Black women (24 percent of them) have ascended to the professional-managerial class."

We saw a glowing example of that ascension depicted on "The Cosby Show" in the eighties when Claire Huxtable, attorney at law, provided a positive and powerful image for young girls. The image is still powerful now as the show remains in heavy syndication.

However, there are still so many images that don't make us proud. These media images can and often do still negatively impact the beliefs of young Black girls. Consequently, even with social, professional and economic gain, some may still be plagued by the belief that they can't be as successful as their Caucasian peers or don't meet what they believe or have been told is the societal standard of beauty. Or they can be impacted by the types of comments Don Imus made about the Rutgers University Women's Basketball team. The negative images in music and videos don't help either. Young Black girls may not believe in themselves or their self-worth.

If you think that we have *overcome* to the point that we are far removed from the color issues illustrated in the now infamous 1940s experiment, which documented Black youths picking White dolls over Black dolls, there are those who beg to differ. Kiri Davis, a New York high school student, made the news recently when she reproduced psychologist Kenneth's Clark's 1947 test and reached the same conclusion. The Black children she captured in her short film, "A Girl Like Me," picked a White doll over a Black one.

We believe that how you feel about yourself will determine how far you can go in your chosen profession. You can't *work it* if you don't have a healthy relationship with yourself. If you think your nose is too big, your hair is too kinky, you're not smart enough, you are inferior, or you can't expect more out of life than being a rap video vixen—you won't excel! High self-esteem isn't arrogance; it's a confidence in yourself and the skin you're in. It is fueled by the belief that you deserve to win!

Lisa Harden Fields, a senior quality engineer in Detroit, Michigan who landed a position where she was the only female and only minority in management agrees, *"If I didn't have high self-esteem I wouldn't succeed in my work environment."*

We decided to feature two Black women with different and compelling stories about self-esteem. These stories depict how the issue of self-esteem impacts lives and careers. The first story describes the journey from low self-esteem to unconditional self-love.

Lisa's Story:

"My self-esteem problems probably began even before I started school. My father walked out on us when I was only four years old. This was after physically abusing my mother in front of us for so many years. It's sad to say, but even as far back as maybe two years old, I can remember the abuse. It was horrifying. He left us for another woman and her child. Coincidentally, her child happened to be the same age as me. I remember feeling as if he left me for that child. There was always a sense that some-

thing was wrong with me and from that stemmed a strong fear of rejection and abandonment.

Throughout my life I encountered other experiences that added to my inability to love myself. These incidents inevitably led to extremely low self-esteem and a host of other problems. It was very hard growing up in an African-American family during the seventies and the eighties. It was a time that, I believe, our culture tended to be totally caught up in hair and skin color. I just happened to be the darkest of my parents' children. I always felt like a fish out of water because I was so much thinner than my sisters. The so-called hallmark of an African-American woman was supposed to be that she was well-endowed in most, if not all, areas. I wasn't. I was often teased about that at home. That taunting flowed over into school as far back as I can remember.

I grew up in a home where I did not receive much affection. I was the youngest of three girls being raised by my mother. My mother lost her mother to cancer when she was only eight years old. Her father took off just before my grandmother died and abandoned them. Mama was raised by her older siblings and other family members. She was tossed from house to house. Because of this she was very strong and an excellent provider; but, to this day, she is still not a very affectionate person. However, she's a wonderful mother. My father on the other hand, although he was not there, was very affectionate. He hugged us and kissed us whenever he saw us. He always told us he loved us. This may sound like I should have turned out okay. However, the feelings of rejection and being very needy for approval of others still consumed my life.

One of the most hurtful incidents from my childhood happened in middle school. One of my friend's fathers touched me inappropriately. This devastated me because I was only 12 years old. I had been very trusting. This made me feel as if that was all I was good for. I felt that I was not worthy of someone caring about me for me. I thought that I would only be liked for sexual purposes. When I got older I went through a fairly short promiscuous stage that ultimately led me to be sexually inhibited. This incident also shaped a disgust for Black men. It caused me to make gener-alized assumptions about a whole race of men that were simply not true.

I hung out with a clique in high school that was my closest friends. Ironically, I held the same position in this clique that I held at home. Not only was I physically the darkest, in my mind at the time, I was the least attractive and intelligent. These thoughts stemmed from the "redbone mentality" of the 1980's. It didn't help, that I was never asked to the prom. I was never nominated for Homecoming. I was often called horrible names and teased about being so thin. I remember one young man would run through the halls. When he would see me he would say, "Hey Po ASS!" Sadly, I got used to him calling me that and I eventually started to reply with a cordial response and a smile. It wasn't long before friends of mine started picking up on my "wonderful" nickname and began calling me that too. I don't think that anyone ever realized how that hurt me. I don't think I knew either.

When I finally did get a boyfriend it didn't last long. Like most teenagers, there was always some other girl waiting to steal him away. Unfortunately, because of my low self-esteem, I internalized this to mean that there was something wrong with me. She was not as skinny as me, she was not as tall as me, and she was prettier than I was. Ironically, while all of these things were happening to me in the Black community, White girls would approach me and say "I wish I were as small as you." They would say that I could be a model and that my height was a good thing. White boys told me I was cute and had a cute figure. Don't get me wrong, Black people would tell me these things too but I tended to focus more on what the Whites said to me. As if what they said validated that they were nicer and better than my own people. I began to internalize this and believe this with all my heart. It did not help matters when I was publicly dumped by a Black guy for a very beautiful White girl.

I do believe that this is when the internal thoughts began to affect my external appearance. I started to try to change the way I dressed and wore my hair. I even went and purchased a pair of blue eyes (contact lenses). This would be the beginning of a long growing process for me and I didn't even realize it. After this, I never even looked at another Black man. I started to date a lot, never really having a serious relationship because I only dated White guys. None of them could take me home to mom and dad. My self-esteem was so low that I didn't feel I deserved to meet their parents. I felt as if I should be hidden.

I never really had anyone to encourage me on goals and dreams. There was no one on either side of my family that was college-educated. Most of my encouragement came from outsiders. Many of those outsiders were White people because I had surrounded myself with them just to feel good about myself. It was having the opposite effect. The more I was around them; the more I felt inferior and the lower my self-esteem dropped.

It was not until I was in high school that I even considered that I would go to college. My mother never talked about it with me. When the subject came up she said she couldn't afford it. So, in my own way, I accepted that I would not go to college. When I did get the opportunity to go, I came back home after only three days. I didn't have the money, or should I say, I did not have the drive to acquire the funds needed to pursue my education.

It took me years of depression and self- pity to realize that I actually did have low self-esteem. I had a child at 19 years old by a young White man. He claimed to love me and was going to marry me. When his parents said "we don't want those Niggers in our family," I got a Dear John letter. I was seven months pregnant and never saw him again. It was not until I was about 22 years old that it finally hit me. I had been through a string of bad interracial relationships before realizing that I couldn't expect anyone to love me until I learned to love myself. I continued to date outside of my race. A revelation came over me that was only the beginning of my transformation. I took a look at myself and actually realized that there were things in me that I needed to work on. That did not happen overnight.

From age 19 to 22 I had partied so hard that I often look back and think about how much of my first son's baby years I missed. Thank God for my mother, because even though I was out on my own, she helped me a great deal. In December of 1991 I decided it was time to grow up. I slowed the partying down and began to be a real parent to my son. I decided in 1992 to turn my life around. Ironically, I was dating a wonderful young White male whom I still feel, to this day, really cared about me. He, too, was caught up in the stigma of the South and what people thought. Ultimately this brought me to the realization that no matter how much these White boys said they loved me, deep down inside, they always felt that they had more to lose than gain by dating me.

My revelation started with me realizing that on the inside I was good person. On the outside I was beautiful. The sad part is that I had modeled for years but I never knew that on the outside I was not ugly or unattractive. It was not until I learned to love myself that I was able to look at my own people and realize how blessed I was and what a beautiful race of people I come from. I started to research my people and my history. I found out so many wonderful things about the Black race and then began to question why I did not learn these things in school. I began to feel proud to be a Black woman! I realized that the Brothers were fine and I had deprived myself of knowing and loving my people for many years. It was time for a change.

I realized that I had wasted years of my life not loving myself. When I looked in the mirror I saw that I was wasting my intelligence and enrolled in college again. This time I was determined to finish. I decided to get the first degree that I had missed out on and acquire a second one. I knew that a double major would take discipline but I was ready for it.

At the time I was dating a young Black male who was very dominating and intimidating. When the drama started in our relationship my personal transformation allowed me to let go. I knew my education was more important. I was celibate for four years, graduated at the top of my class, and was even asked to speak at the ceremony. I had finally learned to love myself. There were times when past events and decisions crept back up to haunt me but I had to realize that I could not control other people and their actions. I could only control how I reacted to them.

For years I covered up my true physical beauty with long flowing hair weaves and colored contacts. I wore them before they actually were in style *or just the trendy thing to do. My preconception that White was better led me to wear those things. It was not until I finally learned to love myself that the fake eyes were discarded. The hair took a little longer because it had become my security blanket. I still suffered from issues of being thin and felt as if the long hair took away from people noticing how thin I really was. While I was in college I found out that I had a thyroid condition called Graves Disease and that, besides having good genes, was one of the reasons I was so thin. I was treated for this condition and went into remission. I then decided to grow my own hair. All of a sudden I did not have to have the hair anymore. The only time I would wear it was if I wanted to. I no longer felt I needed to. Now I wear it every now and then because the look has become a part of me. However, it no longer represents who or what I am. The blue eyes were a bit extreme and I have never touched them again.*

Today I am a different person. I am a born again Christian. I am married and gave birth to a second son who is now five years old. Marriage has not been easy, but it is also a part of the growing process and I have found myself returning to the old lessons learned drawing on the strength that I gained from them in an ongoing attempt to love myself and those around me unconditionally. Perseverance has helped me to handle many hurdles in life. I have found that it can be a never-ending battle to actually focus on what I really want out of life. I am a registered nurse. I also have a bachelor's degree in psychology, a master of science degree in business management. I am currently working toward starting my doctoral degree in nursing. My husband and I recently built our dream home in a city about an hour away from where we grew up. In my career I am currently a nurse administrator at a children's psychiatric hospital for children ages 5-12, but I am still pushing for that top executive position. Ten years ago you couldn't have told me that I would be where I am today. I love and respect all people. Most importantly, I have a love and respect for my people that I never imagined would manifest itself so strongly. In no way is my life perfect. I have realized that this life is a process. I will prob-

ably leave this earth still growing, learning, and attempting to better myself.

I have learned that there is nothing in life that is impossible to overcome or achieve if you just put your mind to it. You can't let others discourage you. You can't make generalized assumptions about people based on what a few idiots do. When you do it can cause you to miss opportunities and people that could be a plus in your life. If you were to miss out on these contacts it could be detrimental to your life, future and career.

I want to tell young ladies, no matter what anyone says, know that you are special just because you are you. Know that you are a survivor just for the fact that you are alive and breathing today. Do not let others make the decision for you on your worth. You are worth more than any mathematical system can create a number for because the important parts of your worth are intangible and abstract; no picture or number exists to describe how wonderful of a person you are. I want young women to know that they should always set their goals very high and know that nothing is impossible. Do not live your life trying to please others or worrying if people like or approve of you. Live your life being someone who you would like, someone you can be proud of, and someone who you can look at in the mirror and say, "I love you because you are beautiful inside and out!"

Lisa T. Williams-Holloway
Columbia, South Carolina
Degrees earned: BSN, BA Psychology, and MS Management
Job Title: Nurse Administrator, Nurse Manager III
Married with two sons

We wanted to share Lisa's story because we think that it is truly inspiring. Her honesty and candor provide a glimpse into her life as she grappled with and overcame her battle with low self-esteem. We are proud of her ability to triumph in her personal life and professional career. She also expressed her journey to self-love through poetry. The following is a poem she wrote in 1996:

167

THE ORIGINAL ARTWORK

My artwork is original, how dare you say it's not?

*There's Sandys, Susans, and Mary Kates, who pay millions to get what
    I naturally got*

There was a time, oh what a time, when my lips were a social sin

But when the ivory woman tried collagen, my lips were suddenly in

They were luscious, and lovely, and oh so beautiful

Hers were not even an act of God, mine are original

*There was a time, Oh what a time, when my ebony people were consid-
    ered 3/5 a man*

But if 3/5 labels the original, then ½ must label a tan

*Would you say that a copy of the Mona Lisa is better than the original
    herself?*

*Then why would the original race on this earth be shunned by everyone
    else*

We are full of color, lips and hips, breast and so much pride

*And through all the slavery, suppression and drugs we've survived the
    genocide*

*You said we were ugly, yet you raped us and loved us when your other
    half would not do*

*So what's the problem, we can't understand, is she not original enough
    for you?*

My pride runs deep, my love is bold

My beauty is elegant young or old

I am a Black Goddess, a Queen, Crown and Dashiki

Wearing and flossing the original works of Cleopatra and Nephretiti

*We were the original Warriors, Kings and Queens, draped in diamonds
    and gold galore*

My artwork is original…need I tell you more?

In 2002, Essence magazine took an active role in encouraging the next generation by featuring a series entitled, "The War on Girls," looking at 'the serious challenges facing our daughters.' A feature from the series, "But Mommy, White Dolls Are Prettier," dealt with teaching your daughter to embrace her own beauty. Ylonda Gault Caviness noted some of the following points in her article:

- As children grow older, parents have to remain consistent in giving those affirming messages of beauty and self-worth.
- African-American girls need to be wrapped in an armor of confidence if they are to weather the White media forces that work to invalidate their beauty and strength as Black women.
- It is foolhardy to think that the negative signals from which we have to safeguard our children come only from White-controlled media. The truth is, some of the most hurtful messages directed at Black children can come from within our own community.

Celebrities are also involved in the effort to help grow young Black girls into successful Black women. In yet another article from "The War on Girls" series superstar Queen Latifah (Dana Owens) lead a discussion with girls about issues of concern and importance to them.

Beyond being bankable at the box office, Latifah is a positive cheerleader for women and girls. Young girls of all colors, shapes, and sizes can be inspired by her success as a Cover Girl model and her Queen Collection. Her acting skills earned her an Oscar nomination. She is the author of *Ladies First: Revelations of a Strong Woman* and *Queen of the Scene*. She is also a businesswoman who appears to have mastered the psychology of success!

On an episode of his now-canceled talk show, Wayne Brady called Latifah the champion of self-esteem.

"I live it!" she responded, explaining that one of the most incredible and sexy things about a woman is her confidence.

"When you carry yourself without self-esteem it allows people to come into your life and take advantage of you," she added.

Our second profile features Dr. Teresa Larke Pope, a school super-intendent in South Carolina who also champions the importance of high self-esteem. Despite early experiences with racism, Dr. Pope was determined to become a role model for racial pride and believes that we shouldn't give others the power to tear us down. Additionally, she shows how she personally passes on this message to our young Black girls and gives advice on how you can do the same. The following is the Work It, Girl! interview with this award-winning educator, mother and wife:

WIG: Growing up in the sixties, what were your experiences with racism? How did those experiences, positively or negatively, impact your life?

TLP: In the seventh grade I experienced my first encounter with racial issues. I had to attend a predominantly White school for the first time. Before this I had never sat in a classroom with White students or had a White teacher. There was no preparation for what I was to endure for the next five years. I went to Jackson High School with no idea of what it would be like. Most White students treated me either as invisible or someone to look down on. The teachers had very low expectations for me and never provided encouragement. The school was very small (70% White/30% Black). I went from being in the top of my class, with a reputation for being academically talented and well liked, to an unknown with very few friends. When I was teased or harassed by White students and reported incidents to the teacher I was always told to sit down. When my frustration turned to tears my principal told me if I came to him crying again he would suspend me from school. It was a hopeless situation and the most difficult years of my life. I chose to endure it and rise above it, planning to show them that I couldn't be held back. My attitude turned this negative situation into a positive learning experience that would give me the motivation to be successful in spite of all the setbacks. I learned from my mother to fight racism by being the best I could be and not letting what others do, who were ignorant as a result of prejudice, cause me to give up and buy into what they thought of me. In essence, I set out to prove the teachers and students of my little school wrong. I also learned that their attitudes were brought on by their lack of knowledge and what they had been taught to believe about people of other races. When I decided to become an educator one of my goals was to change the attitudes of those I would meet by presenting myself as a positive role model...a successful Black female.

WIG: Who was responsible for teaching you to love yourself?

TLP: My mother taught me to take care of myself, to look my best, to speak intelligently, and to value myself as a person. She did this in much the same way that I do for my children. With only an 8th grade education she would correct me if I used poor English, frown on me not looking well groomed, and stressed the value of a good education. She often said people won't treat you right if you don't look like you deserve to be treated with respect. My clothes were always the best she could afford and starched and ironed to perfection as I went off to school. I felt good about myself because I looked good. I had older sisters who loved to see me dressed up. My sister Emma would take me shopping and buy me new clothes. From as early as I can remember, I have made it a habit to dress well. My sister Shirley constantly tried to convince me that being thin was OK because I really struggled with that. Momma told me that one day those who teased me about my size would probably one day be overweight and dieting. She was right!

My sisters and my mother taught me to accept myself, love myself, take care of myself and dismiss the negative comments of those who said I was ugly, skinny, etc. Their words gave me hope at a time in my life when I felt hopeless. This is still something I struggle with because I was a victim of racial slurs and negative put-downs during my school years. Without the support of my mother and sisters this could have been an obstacle that negatively impacted my life. I'll never think of myself as pretty but I will always look professional and well groomed. I'm okay!

WIG: As a mother of three Black girls, how do you instill positive self-esteem and racial pride in your daughters?

TLP: I have always felt that children believe what they see more than what they hear. I model pride and a positive self-esteem. I also use examples from my childhood and my adult life to explain to them that, as a Black female, things will often be unfair. Keeping their faith in God, strong morals and values, along with perseverance and determination, they will be able to hold their heads up high in the face of injustices. I stress to them to feel good about themselves and who they are while keeping a focus on who they will one day become. It's important for them to know that life has not been easy for me and is probably more difficult for them than it is for White females. This is where they should gain their strength. I show them, by example, that I have faced obstacles and continue to face them daily but I keep going. It's a source of pride for me to look back over where I've come from and all the goals I've set and been able to accomplish. I also instill self-esteem and racial pride in my daughters by calling attention to their strengths. My three daughters are very different and I make sure that I don't compare them. I compliment and brag on the good in each one.

WIG: What role does a happy family play in the positive development of children and their outlook on the future?

TLP: There is no perfect household like the one depicted on TV's "Leave it to Beaver" where every day is perfect and every problem is solved in thirty minutes. Families must approach life realistically. In my home we do the best we can. We overcome disappointments and setbacks because we love each other and we have a strong faith in God. A happy family is one who communicates, loves in spite of, accepts failures, celebrates successes, and bears all things- together.

The mother and father show what teamwork can do. They support each other and the children. The parents must show a strong sense of values and morals and live by example. This aids in the positive development of children.

WIG: Can you give us five things parents can do to encourage their children to live their dreams?

TLP: I think these are five things that parents can do:
1. Talk to your child daily. Ask them about their day and truly listen to what they have to say.
2. Offer your children encouragement.
3. Live your life as a positive example for them to follow.
4. Love them unconditionally.
5. Teach them to have faith in God.

WIG: As a former teacher and current administrator, what is your interaction level with young Black girls? What was the percentage of African-American girls at the school that you served as principal of before becoming a superintendent? In what ways were you able to interact with them and assist in their self-esteem development? What is your experience in your new job?

TLP: About 25% of the student body at Redcliffe Elementary was African-American female. I feel that I served as a positive role model for them. Their achievement scores showed that they performed well academically. I didn't single them out but I do feel I had an impact on them from the notes I received saying things such as,' I want to be a principal like you,' 'you look good every day,' 'I like having you as a principal, etc....' When I saw one that may have been struggling I tried to develop a relationship with her so that she could talk to me and change her course to one of success rather than defeat.

In my new role, as the first Black and first female superintendent in the district in which I serve, I see expressions of "Ah!" This is a natural reaction after so many years of seeing only White males in this position. Just as my former students in elementary school did, they like to see what I'm wearing or what hairstyle I have. It's obvious that they are checking me out and if I can impress them enough I know I can convince them to focus on getting their education.

WIG: Your doctoral dissertation dealt with Black and White female administrators. Did it reveal anything to you about the way White women and Black women's backgrounds affect their potential for success? What were your findings?

TLP: My dissertation revealed simply what my mother told me many years ago: Never expect to get the same thing for doing as well as a White person. You have to be better. When she told me this it was in reference to not getting the same attention for doing well in school. Momma saw the unfairness in the grades I received after integration and wanted me to continue to try anyway. She also told me to never compare my work to theirs (Whites in the class) because as a Black female the work I turned in had to be better. So many years later, through my experiences as an educator and in writing my dissertation, the message she gave me has remained relevant. Black women usually have more education and more years of experience in education before receiving an administrative position than White women. With the exception of rare occasions, this still holds true. Black women (based on the research) have more of a desire to pursue advanced degrees and promotions but, even with this motivation, their chances are not as good as the White female. The White female is more likely to be given a position with little effort on her part. There are many factors that lead to this- a major one being that Black females often are the head of the household. Therefore Black females have to work harder, earn advanced degrees and as my mother said 'prove themselves to be better' in order to reach their career goals.

WIG: What role does self-esteem play in success?

TLP: If a person feels like a failure he or she will become one. Life is a self-fulfilling prophecy. You are what you think you are. In school our students become what we expect of them. You get what you expect. Fortunately for some, as in my case, the school can force a negative message in your mind that a strong support group can help you overcome. My mother never let me buy into the low expectations that my teachers in high school held for me. I also had a strong elementary school experience that I could always look back on to know I was capable of much more than the teachers in the 'White' school knew. If you feel you can be successful and you see it modeled in your family you buy into it. And if you believe it, you can achieve it! Valuing yourself is easier when you have people around you who value you as a person as well.

Dr. Teresa Larke Pope is married to George Washington Pope Jr. They are the proud parents of five children. Beyond being an educator, Dr. Pope has always been actively involved in public/community service. She is a member and a former Chapter president of Delta Sigma Theta Sorority Inc. and has been involved in their mentoring programs for young girls. She was actively involved in her children's activities for organizations that include Jack & Jill and Girl Scouts. She has served as president of the South Carolina Alliance of Black School Educators and in leadership roles with the national organization (NABSE). She has devoted her entire professional career to the field of education.

It is important to note that based on our research, interviews and personal experiences we believe that it is virtually impossible for you to experience success without feeling good about yourself. We also believe you can do this and teach others the same by remembering these points:

- Low self-esteem issues are not always a "White" or "society inflicted issue," lack of self-love can start in the home.
- Negative experiences don't have to determine the course of your life. You can overcome low self-esteem.

- Some experiences and life issues may require psychological or spiritual counseling to overcome. If you feel you can't handle issues on your own seek help.
- To get a better understanding of what positive changes you can make in your life read self-help books. There is a wide array of inspirational books, both secular and religious.

Suggested Reading List:

In the Company of My Sisters by Julia A. Boyd

Different and Wonderful: Raising Black Children in a Race Conscious Society by Derek S. Hopson, Ph.D. and Darlene Powell Hopson, Ph.D.

10 Good Choices to Empower Black Women's Lives by Dr. Grace Cornish

The Skin We're In by Janie Victoria Ward, Ed.D.

Girls Hold Up This World by Jada Pinkett Smith

The "Work It, Girl!" Woman:
1) Understands that the road to positive self-esteem starts early. She makes a point to help her daughter(s) and other young girls on their path to self-love. If she's not a mother, she agrees to serve as a mentor.
2) Applauds her own successes, big and small. She knows how to pat herself on the back for a job well done.
3) Understands that although sexism and racism are real problems, they should not control her life and the way she feels about herself.
4) Can look at herself and say, "I Love Me!"
5) Realizes that there is no "perfect" person.
6) Embraces the skin she's in.
7) Understands that having high self-esteem enhances her ability to "work it."
8) Uses her talents, skills and abilities to get what she wants!

The Psychology of Success
Encouraging the Next Generation

This section of the Action Planner is devoted to journaling. Journaling is a great way to connect with your innermost feelings. Find a peaceful place to write and explore your self-esteem.

We should all feel beautiful. Write about what makes you beautiful.

I'm beautiful because:

_____

_____

_____

_____

_____

I feel good about myself when:

_____

_____

_____

_____

_____

The best part of being "me" is:

_____

_____

_____

_____

I can make a difference in young Black girl's self-esteem by:

_____

_____

_____

_____

I love me. Self love is important because:

_____

_____

_____

_____

WORK IT, GIRL! PROFILE OF JANIE VICTORIA WARD

Janie Victoria Ward, Ed.D., is Associate Professor of Education and Human Services and Chair of Africana Studies at Simmons College. The NYU and Harvard educated scholar's teaching, research and outreach have made her a "go to" source for issues of psychology and race. She is the author of The Skin We're In: Teaching Children to be Emotionally Strong, Socially Smart and Spiritually Connected and has written and edited numerous other books, chapters and articles. She is a research associate at the Harvard Graduate School of Education. The authors of *Work It, Girl!* sought out her thoughts on the psychology of success in hopes of encouraging the next generation.

Six Questions For Janie Ward:

1) **WIG:** What role do you believe our self-esteem plays in our road to professional success?

Janie Ward: *Self-esteem plays a very important role and it doesn't really matter which way you cut it. By that I mean that, in some ways you can say that self-esteem is directly related to our ability to be successful because self-esteem is about how we feel about ourselves and our abilities. When we feel good about ourselves and trust our abilities then we can perform well in our professional lives. Conversely, self-esteem is really important especially when it's low and people aren't feeling so good about themselves and they distrust their ability to make it in the professional world. So, either way you look at it, self-esteem plays a very important role in our road to professional success.*

2) **WIG:** What can Black women (mothers, teachers, mentors, relatives) do to empower the next generation?

Janie Ward: *Years ago I wrote an article with a title that I had borrowed from one of August Wilson's plays and it is this idea about cultivating a belief in self greater than anyone's disbelief. I think that that is one of the most important life lessons that we can teach our children. The notion that when you go out into the world, because of who you are and how you look, there are going to be people out there who are going to going to discount you, distrust you and hold you in contempt. That kind of negative energy does a number on you. It can really pull you down and pull you into places that you would not have willingly chosen to go. In order to combat that you have to have a belief in yourself that is far greater than any of their disbelief. You have to have trust in yourself, trust in your instincts and develop the knowledge you need to have to make it in this world. Those things are absolutely critical for children. It all gets generated by, the catalyst for it all, belief in self.*

3) **WIG:** Although racism and sexism are very real issues, how should women try to combat them in their everyday lives?

Janie Ward: *We have to constantly be vigilant and on the lookout for ways in which those 'isms' are undermining us. That said, then I think the question becomes 'how do we do that?' I think there are a huge variety of ways to combat racism and sexism. What we have to do is develop a repertoire of resistance strategies because no one strategy works for every situation. Something that might have worked really well with a boss may not work as well with a co-worker. One of the things you can do is learn how to read any given situation that you are in. Read it for racism. Read it for sexism. By that I mean you have to be really attentive to what's going on and ask yourself, 'what are the patterns that are coming up,' 'where have I seen this before' and 'what are the things that are triggering*

me, evoking a response and pissing me off or making me sad?'
Those are the ways we read situations.

Then I think the second thing we need to do is, if we think it's
about racism and/or sexism, we need to name it. I think we are in
a culture that very carefully tries to convince women that there is
no racism and tries to convince women that sexism is a thing of the
past—you have your freedom now! I think it's a very powerful posi-
tion to be in that you say 'you know what, I trust my judgment on
this one and this is a level of inequality that is race-based or gender-
based and I don't care what anybody else says I'm going to name
it'. Once we name it we free ourselves and we can kick in those
resistance strategies I've talked about.

The third step is to oppose it. Come up with resistance strategies
that work. Some of these resistance strategies are internal, figuring
out what you need psychologically to withstand a situation and
what you need psychologically to think through what you need to
move forward. Sometimes the resistance strategies are more active,
like who do you need to talk to, what letter do you need to write,
and what support do you need to galvanize.

The last thing I call 'replace it.' That is about having the things in
your life that you need to re-energize; things that give you that
energy to go back out there and battle one more day. For some
Black women that is having a rich spiritual life, maybe with the
church or maybe outside of the church. For a lot of Black women
it's about having other women in your life who you can turn to,
who you can cry with, who you can bitch and moan with and say,
'let me tell you what's going on at work!' This allows you to have
someone who can hear you, hear your voice, and offer suggestions
or loving support.

4) **WIG:** Why do many people have a hard time embracing the skin they
   are in?

Janie Ward: *Because we live in a culture that has spent 400 years convincing Black folks that there is something wrong with the skin they're in. So we have this historical legacy. It hasn't gone away yet and we still live with that 400 years of oppression. We were oppressed legally far longer than we have been legally free so it doesn't surprise me at all that we would be still struggling with all the stuff that comes with the skin we're in. We (Black women) have been told over and over again that how we look and the way we present ourselves in the world is just not good enough. The lips are too big, the nose is too wide, the hips are too big and the hair is not straight enough. We have been given a barrage of messages and, again, we have to resist them. We have to stand up and say, "I'm a child of God, and because of that I know that I am as good, as worthy, and as beautiful as anybody else."*

5) **WIG:** What role does home life play in the psychological development of young girls and their outlook for the future?

Janie Ward: *I've often said that home is the primary site of resistance. It's at home where we teach our daughters how to love themselves and each other. It's where we teach our daughters how to resist in ways that are within their control and in ways that are self-affirming and culturally affirming. Those are the lessons that are passed down in homes where things are really working well between parent and child.*

6) **WIG:** What, in your opinion, is the difference between "working" and "working it?"

Janie Ward: *When I think about "working" I think about a task or an activity that has to be undertaken when you work. Sometimes we do that with pleasure and sometimes we absolutely hate doing it. But it has to be done. When I think about "working it" it's a much more active phrase. It speaks to this process of pulling together different pieces, like pulling together a knowledge base and coupling that with your attitude, sort of believing in your ability to get something done. That gets coupled with support, being around people that are saying 'you go girl,' 'you know exactly what you are doing,' and 'it's your time.' Then you put that together with all your hopes and dreams and faith. When all of those things are synchronized and working together and you've got a plan or a purpose, then that is what I would say is "working it!"*

The

"Write"

Tools

The "Write" Tools to Work It, Girl!

It's time to take control of your professional life. In order to do that you have to have the right tools. Today's faltering economy and accompanying competitive job market calls for job hunters to devise strategies and tools that will show employers that they know how to *work it*.

This section will provide you with a sampling of the "write" tools to make that happen. This section contains a *Work It, Girl!* :

- ❖ Power Letter Sample
- ❖ Power Letter To-Do List Sample
- ❖ Resume Sample
- ❖ Resume To-Do List Sample

Then, after you've got the job, we want you to look the part. The "write tools" are followed by the **Work It, Girl! Style Profile** so you can look the part of the successful woman at work!

*Job Scenario A for Power Letter Sample Materials:
Karen Smith is relocating to Charlotte, North Carolina without a job; but, with a solid recommendation as to how to get one. The following cover letter and accompanying To-Do List gives instruction on how she should work it!

*Job Scenario B for Resume Sample Materials:
Professional B. Woman is hoping to secure the Director of Social Work position at a health department. The resume and cover letter provide a sample of how she should work it!

POWER LETTER SAMPLE:

Karen B. Smith
321 North Sunny Way
Some City, Georgia 54321
(153) 321-1563
karenbsmith@workitgirl.com

Mrs. Patricia Edwards
Human Resources Manager
Global HR Concepts, Inc.
1515 The Right Way
City, State 99588

August 18, 2007

Dear Mrs. Edwards,

Vonda Evanson, your former co-worker at HR Stars, recommended I contact you regarding your upcoming project, "Futuristic Human Resources." She and I co-chair the Employment Issues Committee for the American Human Resources Association, and she thought we would make a great team.

I am currently the Assistant Manager of the Employee Assistance Program at Company XYZ. Although I have enjoyed my work there, I plan to relocate to Charlotte this summer and my company has no locations to which I can transfer. My proven track record of developing widely adopted employee services initiatives over the past six years, a master's degree in human resources management and my consistent participation in professional development activities is evidence that I understand the importance of employee needs and can deliver programs that meet them.

Once you have had time to review the resume I included, I would like the opportunity to speak with you regarding the possibility of joining your team. I will call you on the morning of February 25 in hopes of coordinating a time during the week of March 1 that we can meet, if you have not already contacted me. I very much look forward to talking with you and to our potential collaboration.

Thanks for your time and consideration.

Sincerely,
Karen B. Smith

POWER LETTER TO-DO LIST:

Note: How to approach your power letter depends on the circumstances of how you learned about the job. In this instance, (Job Scenario A), there was a referral so the following to-do list is specific to Karen Smith's situation. See the job scenario on the "write" tools introduction page.

Paragraph One: Set the Stage

Name the person who referred you in the very first sentence to catch the employer's attention right off the bat. Then, describe the relationships between all parties involved to establish common ground and further personalize the letter. Even if you don't get the job, the employer may feel more inclined to extend further networking and job search assistance to you.

Paragraph Two: Establish Credentials

This paragraph should make it obvious that you are not looking for a personal favor, but that you are well qualified for the job and would value the professional courtesy of being considered for it. It mentions a few strong points in that regard, rather than re-hashing everything in the resume. It should pique the reader's interest enough to read the resume and pick up the phone to arrange a meeting or to make herself available for a meeting when you call. Finally, don't forget to state something specific you can do for the employer, like '...deliver programs that meet employee needs'.

Paragraph Three: Close the Loop

Re-state your purpose in writing the letter and offer to take the next step, while leaving the door open for the employer to make the next step if she so chooses. It is acceptable to suggest a timeframe for follow-up. If the employer will be unavailable, that might prompt a response sooner.

Remember, how you set the stage, establish your credentials and close the loop will be determined by your specific job scenario.

RESUME SAMPLE: CHRONOLOGICAL FORMAT

Professional B. Woman
123 Business Way
Some City, Georgia 54321
(123) 153-1563
professionalbwoman@workitgirl.com

OBJECTIVE
To obtain the Director of Social Work position at County Health Department.

SUMMARY OF QUALIFICATIONS
- Licensed Clinical Social Worker with 12 years professional experience.
- Five years experience supervising counseling staff and volunteers.
- Outstanding skills in assessing individual, group and program needs.
- Effectively conducts group therapy, seminars, and training.
- Proven record of working with community and professional groups.

WORK EXPERIENCE

Counseling Services Coordinator	August 2000-present

John Smith High School, Atlanta, GA
Administered a state-funded counseling program for at-risk high school students. Provided academic, employment and personal counseling in individual and group settings. Effectively advocated for and coordinated community services and support. Developed individual counseling plans based on skilled assessment. Supervised five counselors and a student intern. Managed an annual budget of approximately $300,000.

Clinical Social Worker	August 1997-July 2000

North Carolina Department of Health
Interviewed adolescents and their family members to determine treatment goals. Effectively maintained a caseload of 150 clients, including records of therapeutic activities and client progress. Served as community liaison to more than 25 local agencies to ensure effective referral services and avoid duplication of services. Annually compiled and edited a comprehensive community resource manual which is used by statewide agencies.

Professional B. Woman
Page Two

Program Specialist   **July 1991-August 1997**
A Better Way Counseling Center, North Carolina
Assisted client population with identifying resources for personal and family care. Conducted health education seminars and arranged for guest speakers on various health and community topics. Developed systems to reduce the backlog of cases and streamlined the processing of new ones. Met regularly with supervisor to evaluate program effectiveness and made recommendations for several changes that have been implemented throughout the company.

EDUCATION
Master's Degree, Clinical Social Work, University of North Carolina   1997
Certificate, Program Development, Community and Family Systems Institute 1994
Bachelor's Degree, Social Work, North Carolina State University   1991

PROFESSIONAL AFFILIATIONS
American Counseling Association member   1997 - present
Advisory Board, The Teen Experience   1998 - present
Volunteer, Kennedy Center for Family Studies   1999 - 2001
Volunteer, Social Programs Committee   1996 - 2000

Resume To-Do List
The Work It, Girl! Resume:

❖ **States specifically what job you want.**

Your objective is to get the job you want. Therefore, your resume should state just that. An effective one is: "To obtain the position of Director of Social Work at County Health Department." Don't get caught up with trying to compose an elaborate statement that isn't a clear statement of your goal, such as: "Seeking a professional opportunity to use my management skills in a company that has much to offer for professional development." Your objective is better stated by communicating that you would like to *get* (obtain) a job, not to *seek* one. Secondly, if the reader has to figure where you belong in the company, he or she may move in to a candidate that better states her fit with the organization.

❖ **Is a work in progress that is tailored to each employer or situation for which it is intended.**

The fact that there is no such thing as 'one size fits all' when it comes to resume writing, does not mean that you will have to start from scratch with each resume you submit. Chances are, you will apply for jobs that are very closely related; therefore, tailoring your resume means "tweaking" each one by using information obtained through networking contacts and clues in each job announcement to make sure your résumé meets all the needs of the employer. With the use of a computer's cut and paste capability this should be no problem at all. On the other hand, there will be times when a more general approach is perfectly acceptable. When circulating your resume during networking contacts for instance, your objective might read: "To obtain a position in the field of social work" rather than "To obtain the Director of Social Work position at County Health Department."

❖ **Summarizes in 4-7 statements that you have what it takes to do the job.**

When a potential employer reads your resume, he or she is trying to narrow the applicant pool. Therefore, the *Summary of Qualifications* MUST demonstrate, without a doubt, that you meet the qualifications of the job. It should include the number of years experience you have in the field, areas of expertise, licenses or certifications, key relevant skills, awards or recognition received, fluency in a foreign language, et cetera. As an added bonus, if you take time to do a great job with this statement, you'll be much better prepared to compose and articulate a face-to-face networking introduction as well as prepare for the highly popular interview request: "Tell me something about yourself."

❖ **Begins every sentence with a past tense, action verb.**

In addition to ensuring conciseness, past tense action verbs help you focus on what skills you bring to the table. For example, rather than: "Responsible for administering a state-funded program" instead state: "Administered a state-funded program."

❖ **Emphasizes how well you can perform by showing the quality, quantity and results of your past actions.**

Once you have completed the first draft of your work experience section, review every sentence to see how you can demonstrate the depth of your experience or what resulted from what you accomplished in that area. For example, specify the amount of the annual budget you maintained, how many clients you served, or the number of staff you supervised. If you streamlined the budget and saved the company thousands of dollars in the process, let it be known! Further, don't forget to mention any of your initiatives that were adopted and any written work that was widely circulated or published.

❖ Includes only the most recent and relevant *professional* information.

Many human resources experts suggest that your resume must not exceed two pages, regardless of how much experience you have. Sticking to the most recent and most relevant information is an effective way to prioritize what goes and what stays if you need to cut back. Personal information like marital status, number of children, hobbies, et cetera, has no place on your resume because they are not relevant to your knowledge, skills and abilities. Finally, avoid use of statements like: "References available upon request." Employers know that you'll provide them if asked.

❖ Is error-free.

Get as many people as possible to review your work. A Sister who knows how to *work it* dots every 'i' and crosses every 't'.

Please note that the resume sample we provided is the chronological format. Others formats include: functional, electronic and the curriculum vitae. A great website to visit for more information on resumes is www.jobstar.com.

"Work It, Girl!"
Style Profile

"Fashion changes but style is timeless."
— Lorraine Morris Cole and Pamela M. McBride, co-authors

Fashion has many meanings. But, for Sisters who work it, fashion means donning the gear that meets the preferred dress standards for the setting in which they **work it**!

The American fashion landscape is an ever-changing scene, often at the whim of what key designers are putting out this year. The fashions they display at events, like New York's Fashion Week, often dictate the trends of the following season. However, many of the designs you see on the runway are not appropriate for the workplace, unless you are a Sister who works in a creative or artistic field that *does* dictate you keep up with these trendy fashions.

So how do you know what is best for your situation? It depends on where you work. There are basically four types of work environments when it comes to on-the-job attire:

CONSERVATIVE: This work environment calls for business attire—namely skirt suits, dresses or pant suits. The conservative dress code is often found in the corporate world and is characterized by business suits in neutral colors like black, navy blue, tan, and brown. Shirts are usually in light solid colors like white, off-white and pastels or have conservative patterns with small prints or pinstripes.

CASUAL: Unlike corporate America, the business suit is not a required part of this work wardrobe. And, although you can add more colors to your outfits, don't go overboard. Fluorescents and the like have no place in the casual work setting. Functional clothing is a mainstay in this category. You'll find more khaki pants and cotton clothes in this environment.

UNIFORM: Although this category leaves little room for variety, it can be the easiest workplace wardrobe to maintain. Typically, under these guidelines, everyone is expected to dress in uniforms, whether provided by the employer, or purchased by the employees. Or, there is a uniform dress code that dictates the colors or types of garments that are acceptable. For example, stylists at an upscale hair salon may all be asked to wear black.

COSMOPOLITAN: This workplace environment can be found in more creative occupations, including entertainment and the arts. For example, you may find a record executive wearing the latest Gucci cape and catsuit ensemble in the office and at her new artist's album release party. Since the nature of their business is conducive to this attire, trendy clothes definitely are a 'go' in this work atmosphere.

Although fashion picks for work are also a matter of taste, affordability and availability, don't believe the hype when it comes to making a lasting impression. The following *"Work It, Girl!"* realities will tip you off to the truths that transcend work environments. And, unlike fashion trends, this information won't go out of style.

STYLES THAT DON'T WORK IT, GIRL!

Short Skirting the Issue:
The now-canceled television show "Ally McBeal" gave rise, literally, to the skirt. It seems as the show's popularity went up, so did the main character's hemline. But this, and other ultra-contemporary topics, including

the storyline content, and the unisex restroom, was not a realistic slice of the mainstream work environment. If you have to pull your skirt down every time you sit down, it's too short or too small.

You're Jingling Baby:

Excessive jewelry can be distracting and noisy. An armful of bracelets are better suited for after work attire. The same goes for bulky earrings that have noisy parts. Beeping watches, ringing cell phones and other noisy high tech gadgets are also a "no-no." Silence can be golden in the workplace.

One Size Fits All:

The one size fits all is not a good deal for workplace clothes. Your clothing should have a tailored look and fit. Although most people don't attempt to wear "one size fits all" on the regular basis in workplace, they do wear clothes that simply don't fit. Sometimes it's the unfortunate result of yo-yo dieting. Going from a size 12 to a size 8 is a major change for your wardrobe. Fortunately, those clothes can be altered to fit. However, some people are unsure that they can maintain their new size and keep the same clothes. The same is true for gaining weight. Squeezing into your size 8 when you know you are now up to a size 10 may feel like a great accomplishment. Unfortunately, it won't look good.

Cocktail Wishes and After-Five Dreams:

You want to live the glamorous life? That's great if your job dictates it. However, coming to work in cocktail clothes and formal accessories in work environments that don't support this level of elegance is not a good idea, especially if you want to be taken seriously.

Casual Friday Crispness:

Many corporations are getting away from "Casual Friday." According to human resources professionals, many employees take advantage of this opportunity to wear clothing that is simply *too* casual, including rumpled clothes, sneakers, jeans, t-shirts and have unkempt physical appearances. Remember that in corporate America "Casual Friday" is a privilege and refers to casual *professional* clothes. Although more casual clothing is acceptable, your attire still needs to be fresh and well kept. If you have the opportunity to enjoy this more relaxed dress code, follow the rules of appropriate casual attire set by your employer. It could be that jeans are allowed; so, when in doubt, check it out!

Shoes Clues:
Shoes have to live up to the outfit. A great suit accompanied by worn or scuffed shoes is not a good match. Nor is it appropriate to wear heels that are so high that you can't function well in them. Some companies don't allow open toe shoes and list them as a safety hazard. When in doubt, check your handbook or ask an HR professional. The shoes rule: Whether fashionable, functional, or both, shoes should be well maintained and appropriate for the workplace.

Design of the Decade Myth:
Janet Jackson's best-selling CD titled *Design of a Decade* doesn't apply to workplace fashion. Unless it's a classic piece, most clothes don't stay current for ten years. Many women hang on to clothes saying, "this fashion will return." Newsflash — fashions do return, but it's never exactly the same garment and it may not fit as well as it did the first time. Update your wardrobe. If you buy trendy pieces, make sure that you recognize when the trend no longer works and when wear and tear dictates that you replace the garments.

Ring Around The Collar:
Another workplace fashion faux pas is stained or unfresh garments. A ring around the collar of your blouse or shirt does not project a professional image. Whether you clean them yourself or put your work clothes in the dry cleaners, it is important to keep clothes clean and fresh.

The Repeat Offender:

Wearing the same outfit noticeably and repeatedly is not a good idea. Image consultants suggest that you can make 30 outfits out of only 11 items. The trick here is to interchange garments and accessories to create different ensembles.

The Replacements:

It's not just a movie title; it is also a good idea for the workplace. Keep replacement items at work. One of the most common items that women need is a back-up pair of neutral or flesh tone pantyhose. Also, an extra shirt among your supplies can remedy a lunchtime spill. But, changing anything beyond a shirt or hose may require a quick trip back home (or to the mall, whichever is closer). Always keep an emergency outfit ready to go in your closet.

The **Work It, Girl!** Woman knows that dress is very important to professional success!

Dear Reader:

You are now an expert on the **Work It, Girl!** concept. You can make **10 Good Choices** to get ahead and be **passionate about your career** while striving to **have it all.** You know how to be a **Jill-of-all-trades** who is also the **mistress of her destiny.** You know that you can **stay put and achieve success without making a move.** You have discovered that **working from home** is a viable and exciting opportunity and you can eventually live for a time when **it's not about the money.** When given the chance to experience the contentment of **turning your hobby into a career** or the chance to marvel at the excitement of being **out on a limb and excelling in a daring and non-traditional career,** you know that the **psychology of success and encouraging the next generation** are important. Most of all, you are equipped to *"WORK IT, GIRL!"*

Lorraine Morris Cole
Pamela M. McBride
Contacts@workitgirlweb.com

About the Authors

Lorraine Morris Cole is a seasoned writer and communications professional. Some of the publications that have featured her work include *Upscale* and *Military Spouse* magazines. Her voice has been heard as a correspondent on National Public Radio (NPR). She writes promotional video scripts and has had poetry published by a national greeting card company. She is credited for nominating the first ever Arabesque Man for BET Books. With over 100 articles published she continues to freelance for various publications. She also presents workshops and seminars around the country, including the popular "Effective Communication Skills in the Workplace." Her professional experience also includes teaching public speaking in continuing education programs. Most recently she added yet another dimension to her career in communications by adding columnist to her list of credentials.

Born in Augusta, Georgia and raised in South Carolina, Lorraine also lived in Norfolk, Virginia and Doraville, Georgia before marrying her husband Brian, a military officer. Since then she has lived in Kansas, North Carolina and currently lives outside of Washington, D.C. in a suburb of northern Virginia with her husband, stepson Brian Jr. (BJ), and children Hayley and Evan Cole.

A graduate of Norfolk State University she earned a bachelor's of science degree in mass communications.

Her favorite professional pursuit is any project that empowers women.

Pamela McBride has provided extensive individual career counseling and countless career management workshops during her more than fourteen years of experience in the career counseling field. In the mid 90's she parlayed that experience into the world of writing as a freelance writer and editorial consultant and quickly racked up more than 100 articles published nationally. For several years she was a frequent contributor to the "Work and Wealth" section of *Essence* magazine, *Black Collegian, Upscale,* and *Army Times* publications. Her work has appeared in *Black Enterprise, Military Spouse* magazine, and various online publications. She was also selected as a columnist for the Honolulu *Star-Bulletin* and has accepted invitations as guest speaker to share her insight on professional, education, and personal development.

Pamela now manages multi-million dollar programs and contracts with a leading firm that provides professional and technical services to government and business clients. She has a Bachelor's Degree in Business Management and Spanish, as well as a Master's Degree in Community Counseling. She is a member of the National Association for Female Executives and the American Management Association.

Pamela was born and raised in Boston, Massachusetts but has also lived in Texas, Maryland, North Carolina, Virginia, Rhode Island, Hawaii, and now Georgia with Doug, her Army husband of 18 years (a Lieutenant Colonel in the U.S. Army), her son Tré, and daughter Taylor.

Parker Publishing, LLC

Celebrating Black
Love Life Literature

Mail or fax orders to:
12523 Limonite Avenue
Suite #220-438
Mira Loma, CA 91752
(866) 205-7902
(951) 685-8036 fax

or order from our Web site:
www.parker-publishing.com
orders@parker-publishing.com

Ship to:
Name: _____

Address: _____
_____

City: _____

State: _____ Zip:_____

Phone: _____

Qty	Title	Price	Total

Shipping and handling is $3.50, Priority Mail shipping is $6.00
FREE standard shipping for orders over $30   Add S&H

Alaska, Hawaii, and international orders – call for rates   CA residents add
7.75% sales tax

See Website for special discounts and promotions   Total

Payment methods: We accept Visa, MasterCard, Discovery, or money orders. **NO PERSONAL CHECKS.**

Payment Method: (circle one):   VISA   MC   DISC   Money Order

Name on Card: _____

Card Number: _____ Exp Date: _____

Billing Address: _____
_____

City: _____

State: _____ Zip:_____